AF413773

How One Teacher Came of Age
and Inspired the Next Generation

ANDEE M. NUNN

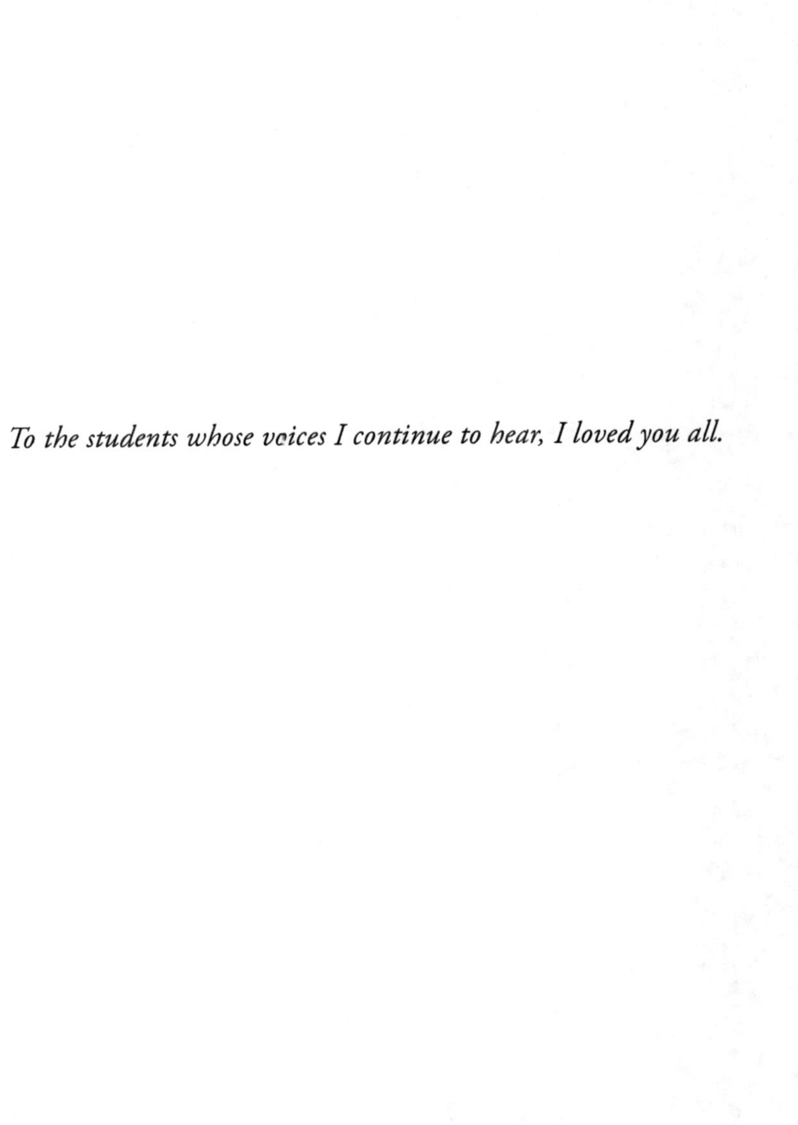

To the students whose voices I continue to hear, I loved you all.

Acknowledgments

I began this project seventeen years ago when I reunited with Forrest, the first student who influenced my life and helped mold me into a teacher. His presence in my classroom determined my future as an educator. Although he walks with angels now, he accompanied me year after year into every classroom. I remember him daily.

Without the support and constructive criticism given by my sister, Maxine, this project would still be sitting in various folders scattered on my desktop. She understood my need to share not only my story, but also, the stories of so many who sat in my classes. I will always be grateful for the endless hours of help. Mommy often suggested that I depend on Max for academic assistance, but as a child, I was stiff-necked and refused to heed her direction until now. Mothers are always correct.

Brooklyn Principals Adolph Dembo and Barbara Williams, who supported me and my growth as I stumbled my way into becoming an effective educator.

My Danbury High teaching partners: Joe Vas, Bonnie Lieberman, and Doug Goodrich. Together we made learning fun and memorable. Each one of you added a different flavor to the room.

Two special colleagues and friends: Hala Hourani, whose instruction and direction helped me tackle and teach more intricate poetry. I will always love "The Flesh and the Spirit" and Tom Agnes, whose unequalled dry wit aided in coping with incomprehensible administrative directives.

My editor, Candi Cross, believed in me and encouraged me to follow through with my ideas. I am grateful.

My parents, Freda and Sol Phillips who supported my most important life decisions. Mommy, a virtuous woman, and Daddy, my gentle giant walked a different path with me, and I am grateful for their devotion.

Throughout the writing process, my husband, Ronnie, patiently and repeatedly listened to stories and reinforced the need for others to hear and understand what makes a class memorable. With his prior teaching experience, he offered pointers that made sense. He is always my critic but also, my best fan, my adored partner. I entered the "forbidden door" and married him, my best life decision.

To my successful daughters, Ilana and Alexi, to whom I passed the "motherhood baton", they will always be my besties. Both are raising future leaders who celebrate equity, diversity, and inclusion like their parents. Thank you for your fruits: Adaeze and Nnamdi Okafor and Cheyson and Charley Freeman. I wear their names etched in silver around my neck and keep them near to my heart. They fill me with such joy and make aging so much sweeter.

To all my students in Brooklyn and Danbury: I learned to be better at my craft because of you. I heard you; I listened to your voices. No one loved you more, and I miss all of you.

Preface

"When a story is told, it is not forgotten. It becomes something else—the memories of who we were, the hope of what we can become."

—*Tatiana de Rosnay*

AFTER RETIRING FROM full-time teaching, writing becomes cathartic. It allows images of amazing young people who left imprints on my heart to be revisited. The group is only a sampling of the souls who affected my teaching, taught me empathy, and changed my life's purpose forever. This is not a heavily researched project, but more a documentation of personal experiences, as well as the produced works from my classroom. It's been quite a journey of learning and reflecting upon those who sat in the seats both in New York and Connecticut. It begins when I was as a naïve twenty-two-year-old newbie in Bedford-Stuyvesant, Brooklyn and ends in Danbury, Connecticut, where I recently served as a parttime adjunct faculty member at Western Connecticut State University, for I was not yet ready to permanently close the classroom door or walk away from education.

The idea of becoming a teacher started long ago in 1953 at age six in my imaginary classroom that I created in my basement. However,

I never fathomed that I would morph from the make- believe teacher into a successful educator who could transform the lives of her pupils. That never would have been possible without the thousands of students who impacted who I would become. Daily, I learned from the faces that stared back at me. Each day was different; each day I made adjustments and initially, I barely survived.

I share the following memoir to prove that a little girl's dream of teaching became a reality. The pages are filled with my words, my recollections and more importantly, the words of my students from middle school, high school, and college. If, like me, you listen to their voices, you too will be permanently changed by the magical exchange.

Chapter 1

RAISED ON LONG Island by protective parents, I knew little of the outside world. My fairy tale childhood outwardly was representative of the 1950s suburban family fulfilling the so-called American Dream.

At age five, the family uprooted from Bensonhurst, Brooklyn, my daddy's birthplace, when he purchased a small ranch-style home in Valley Stream, Long Island, one of the first bedroom communities outside the city boundary. My father and my mom's niece bought adjacent homes, and I grew up developing a special relationship with my cousin, Stellie, and her family. My mother adored her niece, and her niece adored me. A special bond began when I was a baby and being a significantly older first cousin, she babysat for me. For years, her family remained next door and became an extension of my own home as I bounced back and forth.

My mother, a stay-at-home mom, spent her days cleaning, cooking and after a few years of keeping house and raising daughters, she became a shopping pro, scanning bargains at the trendy Green Acres shopping mall, a new local attraction typical of the era. My dad traveled daily to the Bronx where he initially was a furniture buyer for Paris Decorators. Eventually, he decided to become his own boss and with a partner, built a small trucking service, White Line, which delivered goods purchased from New York furniture stores, including his old stomping grounds, Paris Decorators.

I was firstborn of two girls. The position led me to become the bossy one whose sole purpose was to torture my sister, Maxine. I couldn't comprehend how polar opposite we were and got frustrated when she didn't want to play princess or school with me. I loved to dance and listen to 45" records, but she wasn't the least bit interested. Sometimes just to be belligerent, I turned up the victrola volume, causing her to close her bedroom door. Whether I reveled performing ballet, pointe or tap at recitals, she wanted no part of it and I found nothing to unite our diverse interests. Instead of enjoying time with my sibling, I reached out to a couple of girls on the block and avoided Max. Since I rarely ventured off the block, my friends and I tried to find ways to stay occupied even when we often claimed boredom. I didn't like sports, which eliminated lots of games, and I hesitated learning how to ride a bike until I was too embarrassed not to at about ten years old. Summers were better though since our above-ground pool became a refuge from June through August.

It didn't help my self-worth that little sister was extremely intelligent, mastering all classes every year with straight-A grades and honors-course placements. I battled learning math and science, settling for overall B grades and protesting my mom's suggestion that Max tutor me since that idea caused major humiliation. For years, I couldn't erase my recurring nightmare about failing Biology, and it permeated my brain causing me to wake in cold sweats. Yet, somehow, I squeaked through the Regent exams and breathed with relief. My overall GPA was fine when the calculation included my A grades in English, Spanish, History, and Music. However, I recall feeling devastated when although I was a candidate, I was rejected from entrance into National Honor Society at a surprise induction assembly. I sat that morning in the school auditorium waiting for the names to be announced in alphabetical order. I heard the administrator echo: Peter Passalacqua, *pause*, and then Gary Quartararo, skipping "Phillips" and it was over for me. It reinforced my feeling of academic inadequacy that etched in my brain for quite a while.

I was a daddy's girl. I mirrored his personality, silly sense of humor, and his genetics. I just looked like a Phillips, and that wasn't a bad thing at a time when women's worth was judged more by beauty than brains. On the other hand, my sister was different. She and Mommy spent endless hours fighting, as my mother tried to transform her into a girly girl, something she vehemently rejected.

Because of Mom's behavior, I rarely played outdoors after school. Mom's manic side insisted that I return home, undress, transfer my school clothes first into the washing machine then dryer. Eventually they were folded and rehoused in a specified drawer or placed in my closet, where pants hung like soldiers all disguised by plastic coverings that kept them in order but difficult to distinguish. Daily, I showered before 4:00 p.m., so, I was not like others my age who played outside after 3:00 p.m. during the week. I followed Mom's directives and focused on homework completion rather than recreation. At the time, it was all I knew so it didn't bother me, but later in life when my husband questioned me about after-school activities, I realized that the bizarre behavior prohibited me from exploring activities, sports, and clubs I might have enjoyed.

Despite Mom's unreasonable behavior and demands, I was basically a happy person. I conceded that "Max", as she preferred to be called, was inherently smarter. While I struggled and complained about assignments, Max achieved high honors and scholarships. It was an irritant.

When I could, I ignored Mom's erratic actions and even challenged her by being spiteful or playful when she was serious. If she demanded I clean up an already immaculate room, I purposely dumped my laundry into an unavoidable pile rather than arrange it in my color-coded drawers. Unevenly matched, my humor often won for the moment, but my mother's OCD behaviors remained. Looking back, many of her rules and antics were irrational, but they were part of my normal. Monthly, I found her standing on top of the dining room table, trusty rag and Windex in hand, as she cleaned chandelier crystals, one by one, until each sparkled with rainbow hues. The stove and refrigerator received the same treatment and appeared unused. Years later, I discovered that my mom's vacillating behavior was the product of a family genetic trait given a new label: bipolar 2. Bottles of Lithium and Effexor stabilized my mom's mental illness.

Both parents instilled a work ethic early and insisted Max and I find summer jobs to teach us accountability. I recall as kids, a summer when we traveled to the Bronx with Dad, who got us jobs stuffing, licking and sealing envelopes at one of his customer's businesses. We earned $35 per week. By the time taxes were subtracted and we purchased food at a local luncheonette, we went home with less than half our earnings. According to Dad, we would learn to be responsible. Even when my net pay was next to nothing, I worked.

Throughout junior high school, I suffered preteen angst that challenged my self-image. Desperately in need of dentistry, braces finally corrected my hideous overbite. My teeth, which previously jutted perpendicular to my gums and never permitted me to smile comfortably, were rearranged in perfect order by orthodonture. My untamed frizzies relaxed, courtesy of new improved hair products and the invention of a hair dryer. Hours of haircare made a remarkable difference. And thankfully, some excess baby-weight vanished. Why not seek acknowledgement for my improved physical appearance? It made sense to me because it also represented my new position in the family. I often was acknowledged as the "second-best looking" Phillips ranked slightly under my cousin, Susan, whose looks crossed between Natalie Wood and Liz Taylor. Although I dismissed my dad's remark, "Andee has my beauty and Max has my brains," it left its mark. Need I embellish?

By high school, my social life significantly changed as my later teen years were rewarding. Even though most of our community was comprised of people of Italian or Irish descent and mom prohibited me from dating outside my faith, I secretly rebelled. I lied but was not very convincing and usually got caught. I maintained a few clandestine relationships probably out of spite, but they were harmless—a movie, an occasional mall meeting and once, a dalliance at the World's Fair in Flushing with a guy Mom labeled "a bad boy". We bumped heads when my indiscretions were discovered. Mom was livid, threatening to leave home. Once she dramatically disappeared, suitcase in hand, to demonstrate the seriousness of my actions, but then returned with her empty luggage to her crying daughter's remorse. I survived the taboo relationships and frankly, never acted too inappropriately. Like Eliza Doolittle, I was a good girl. Popularity became my middle name; during my senior year, classmates voted me "Friendliest" as indicated in my class yearbook and I also received nominations for: Miss Central High School, Prettiest Senior, and Prom Queen. After all, these were the priorities for a typical high school girl at the time.

Disappointedly, I settled for runner-up in most categories. A wonderful person, Marilyn B. was elected both Miss Central and Prom Queen. Her involvement in extracurricular activities and community service were unequalled. The "Prettiest" superlative went to Pam S., a statuesque, thin schoolmate whose outstanding turquoise eyes were magnetizing. After graduation, she became a Candy Jones model. So, my losses were fair but as a teen, my priorities and ego were unbalanced.

Throughout teen years, the house summer work mandate resurfaced, and I sought parttime employment from June through Labor Day. When I wasn't swimming in the backyard pool or enjoying Jones Beach, West End 2 with friends, I was working. Whether assisting in an office or selling junior wear at local retail stores, I worked. Green Acres Mall offered numerous opportunities and I jumped at the chance to work in Gimbels, a Macy's competitor at the time, along with Alexanders, another popular anchor store. Although I was learning to be a responsible person, I admit to spending much of my wages on jewelry, make-up, or hair goods. While Max built her bank account, my earnings depleted quickly.

Boyfriends were never a problem. In the 60s, if a guy desired a Saturday night date, he called me by Wednesday night, a sign of respect. That was protocol. I always had a boyfriend, some for weeks, others for months with one special "Jonathan" who weaved in and out of my life for years. Mom liked some, disliked others usually to keep me sheltered from hurt and disappointment. I understood her, half listened to her but truly did not heed her directives. This was before the sexual revolution of the late 60s. I was not sexually active (something she didn't believe) so there were truly no worries for her, but I did push her buttons by occasionally dating a "bad boy" despite her warnings. Her warnings became a reality check when one boy's parent called me a "kike", a derogatory term for Jew that was never part of my vocabulary or prior knowledge. It was never about religion; I simply thought the guy was cute but not too smart and a bit too boring. Yet, that situation was eye-opening and reinforced my mother's belief to "stick with my own kind", a phrase I later heard in the movie, "West Side Story", when the lovely Latina Maria liked a white boy. My dalliances were harmless, but I became more cautious after the hurtful, unwarranted name-calling incident. In my opinion, I enjoyed the high school fairy tale adventure in my protective Long Island environment. Movie dates, followed by French fries and a coke at the local diner, consumed my weekends and with a driver's license earned at seventeen, I denied myself little and just enjoyed the teenage "Happy Days" ride. But then, Paradise lost.

After high school graduation, my ideal life vanished. *Poof!* Forced to commute to Queens College, I resented my daddy's assumption that although my outer wrapper was, in his eyes, outstanding, I didn't have the inner goods to pursue an education away from home. After all, I was a social butterfly who occasionally tested him by bringing the wrong guy home, drinking once at a school dance, or lying over nonsensical kid stuff, so he assumed I'd waste his money. Would I even complete college, or would I just meet some guy and get married? So, as my friends prepared for new journeys on campuses all over the country, I mourned my inevitable destiny. It was unfair that two years later, even Maxine would enjoy Cornell's dorm life. I yearned for the campus/dorm experience but was denied the chance and ironically, Max preferred to stay home but that was also forbidden. For me, my life stunted in a flash.

Instantly at Queens College, New York, my popularity disappeared as I became a number in a sea of numbers where I begrudgingly tried to make the best of an awful situation. Given a red Sunbeam Alpine sportscar was my compensation and supposed to appease me. *Wrong.* I drove around forever searching for parking and repeatedly ran late to classes until Dad literally rented a parking spot at a local gas station. I know that I sound spoiled, but all my friends were gone enjoying the college experience and learning how to live on their own. Insecure, I hooked onto a new boyfriend, and I robotically completed semester after semester searching for happier times.

Four years felt like an eternity. I hated college, I hated the student body comprised predominately of students from Queens' high schools who never made me feel welcomed and I hated the daily drive from Long Island. Mom thought I would be comfortable amongst the large Jewish population, but she was so wrong. I was miserable with no niche. Year after year, I drove the ninety-minute commute back and forth to a college that afforded commuters insufficient extracurricular activities and no dorm life—just an inexpensive education.

In four years, including two summer sessions because I couldn't bear a semester more, I earned a B.A. with a Communications/Speech major and Education minor, as well as certification to teach in the New York school system. My success included juggling student teaching placement due to a teacher's strike that could have delayed my graduation, but I refused to elongate the four-year torturous stay and got the job done. (I immediately presented proof of my accomplishment, a Xerox copy of my certification, to Dad. Eventually, he received additional proof as I later earned the official credentials of Master's Degree in Education, Certification in Elementary Education, English in High Schools and as a Licensed Reading Specialist.) I proved that I could handle academic rigor, and I tried to demonstrate that I earned what he thought could never be mine.

By May 1969, right after graduation ceremonies, I was searching for a job. My family knew entering the workforce was the next step, no breather permitted. I was elated to leave the university, wiping my feet, and initially planned never to look back.

Securing a job offered a new set of problems. Ironically, positions for English teachers were plentiful, but finding one for someone licensed in Speech in the High School was like looking for my mother's missing contact lens on a hotel room floor! (A prior experience that ended in failure and rug-burned knees.) My parents expected me to gain employment and instilled the importance of productivity at an early age. So, upon graduation, my folks expected that I earn my keep, live at home, and contribute to the household expenses. The rules: pay bills on time, do not over-buy and never pay a penny interest on any credit card! If you cannot afford it, leave whatever it is in the store. These were Dad's life lessons in responsibility that I still abide by today.

Every morning, I scanned the classifieds of our local paper, *Newsday*, searching for something so Daddy's unsettling looks would be replaced with hopeful grins. And one morning, a temporary, possible solution stared back at me. The ad read, "Wanted: Drama instructor, Merrick Woods summer day camp. 8 weeks, $600. Start 7/05. Call for interview." Eager for me to get settled, my father volunteered to dial the number when my fingers didn't move the rotary disc fast enough. Granted a meeting later that day, I sat before Adolph Dembo, the camp director, who interviewed and hired me in minutes. Summer employment was solidified. This position could delay my concern about September plans. Yet throughout the interview, Dembo's questions focused primarily on my teaching status rather than the duties and requirements of this parttime position.

Within seconds, after signing the camp contract, he blurted, "It's May. What are you doing until July?"

"Waiting for graduation day next week and looking for a permanent teaching position," I responded. My résumé in his hand, he noted my credentials and my mission statement. After moments of perusal, he scribbled something on a pad, tore off the message and pushed it across the table.

"Here. I'm a principal in Brooklyn. You'll make more money in June substitute teaching one month than working here the entire summer at camp—$40 a day, and if you can handle it, you'll have a job for September." That calculated to a minimum of $800 and possibly $1000, I thought. With that he nodded, I nodded back, he rose, pointed towards the piece of paper, shook my hand, dismissed me, and left me to read his notations: "Brooklyn, JHS 35, 272 McDonough Street, crossing Lewis...9:00 am Monday, bring file number."

Stunned and slightly enthusiastic, this almost twenty-one-year-old returned home and in a boastful manner, reported gainful summer employment, as well as a substitute teaching job with a possible fall career opportunity. No hiatus, instant work plans. My parents' reactions were contradictory. Mommy, content with the summer work, heard the location of the teaching position, mumbled something in Yiddish that hinted it might not be a good idea to pursue substituting. Daddy, on the other hand, waved a hand, shutting her down.

"Let her go. She'll learn." With that, he ended the rebuttal, and I knew I was employed. I knew nothing about Brooklyn, especially Bedford Stuyvesant. My father, who helped me with directions since there was no Waze 1969 edition, assured me it was about a thirty-minute drive mainly on the Interboro Parkway (later renamed the Jackie Robinson Parkway). The drive was closer to an hour—without traffic.

After a sleepless Sunday night, on Monday morning dressed to impress, I drove to work in my red convertible sportscar. Fifty-five minutes later, after passing boarded up, graffiti-covered housing and scores of idle people sitting on stoops or hanging on street corners, I parked down the street from this old brick building, a place that would be my second home for the next ten years.

Numerous films broach the difficult subject of teachers untrained to work in areas labeled low socio-economic districts, unfamiliar with the students in difficult school settings starting with "Blackboard Jungle" where actor Glen Ford reluctantly learned to "tame" juvenile delinquents, and "To Sir with Love" where an adult Sidney Poitier mastered the art of teaching in the slums of England. Hollywood thrived as audiences marveled at clueless actress Sandy Dennis's performance in "Up the Down Staircase", which reinforced the problem. Years later, scores of movies still tackle the subject. There are a few success stories such as the portrayal in the book, *Freedom Writers*, but for many fish out of water, the issue continues as it did when I entered teaching. The lesson: educate yourself about your students if you do not want failure.

Regardless of how many courses one takes to prepare for teaching, one has no clue how to address the fires until dropped into the oven.

With my innocence on the line, professional briefcase in hand, I scampered up steps, scanned the building before me, clasped the handle of the cold, steel front door and entered a foreign place, a new world with no experience and no bag of tricks.

Chapter 2

IN THE SPRING of 1969, I felt equipped to embark on my teaching career in Brooklyn's Bedford Stuyvesant. Armed with the knowledge acquired from multiple undergraduate education courses, I marched into the building, Stephen Decatur JHS 35, believing I was prepared. After all, Queens College, a reputable institution of learning, required its education students to complete a plethora of courses that included onsite observations and participation hours, in addition to my whirl-wind student teaching semester that, ironically, took place during the New York City teachers' strike. Determined to complete course requirements, despite the chaos of the time, I bounced from Martin Van Buren High School, Queens to Valley Stream Central, my Long Island high school alma mater, then back to Van Buren to document work hours until the teacher walkout ended. At the time, 1969, I believed that I absorbed enough, was provided with a solid foundation, knew the basics, and was equipped for classroom challenges.

After a night of tossing and turning, anticipating the parkway ride and traffic issues, I began the journey early and arrived about thirty minutes before expected. Being prompt for appointments was a familial trait and this opening day was no different.

I parked a few blocks from the school entrance, checked out my appearance in the car mirror, and nodded to reassure myself. Although nervous tension accompanied me when I walked through the windowless double doors in June 1969 to assume the position of daily substitute, I felt invincible. Dressed in a crisp tan summer weight suit, as well as low-heeled sandals to match, I donned a fresh haircut. After all, this was my first day of school! Since impressions matter, I carried a rich brown leather attaché case bursting with sample lesson plans written in accordance with Board of Education standards. Eagerly, I felt prepared to engage learners by sharing unique strategies, the newest ideas and motivational questions that crowded my brain. My internal voice whispered, "You've got this!" Day one commenced.

After more than fifty years, I still recall the sights that consumed me on day one. I stepped into an old, clean brick building housed between brownstone homes most in need of repair. The building's interior was bordering on decrepit, dark, and unappealing contrary to Central High School, my alma mater that bragged of its lakefront property and sprawling green lawn. Preteens blocked the entrance as I wiggled my way through a crowd busy socializing and reluctant to move aside for my passage until the warning bell blared.

On my way to the main office, I curiously peered into open-door classrooms that were far less appealing than I envisioned: locked steel windowless doors, stark celery green painted walls, grey steel garbage pails, old chalkboards without erasers, and bland bulletin boards empty of eye-catching student work or motivational posters. The individual desks etched and carved with names and doodled designs, held chewing gum residue on their undersides. *Not very inviting*, I thought, as my creative side imagined a transformation, an inviting, warm environment that would celebrate learning.

After a perusal of the surroundings, I followed arrows and wiggled my way a short distance to the main office. Faculty members bustled, coming and going, punching timecards, emptying mailboxes, greeting one another, and then gone leaving at least ten adults waiting for schedules and direction. I heard shout-outs of names as the slew of substitutes simultaneously received their daily assignments. I learned that many teachers hoarded sick days to use during June's final weeks when kids were antsy, waiting for the end of the school year and oppressive indoor heat reinforced the lure of running outdoors. The inside air remained motionless despite fans dispersed in four corners of the main office. Even when humidity eventually decreased, thick air stubbornly remained, as this building did not let the stifling heat dissipate.

After the line diminished, I took a deep breath, searched for a less harried secretary, and introduced myself. She had been expecting me and with barely an acknowledgement, she handed over a clipboard, pen, and stack of paperwork to complete and pointed me towards an empty bench. Sitting, it took me some time to complete forms thankfully with the mandatory file number in hand.

Startled by the blare of the homeroom bell, I witnessed the hallways flood with movement as a disparate group of young people dispersed. They came in all shapes and sizes; some carried books while others were empty handed. Many shouted, ignored inside voices, a few scurried while others sauntered and disregarded the authority figures planted at designated locations like stairwells and bathrooms to manage crowd control and keep the masses moving. After a third bell, halls generally cleared, leaving just a few stragglers and a rare substitute still searching for a specific classroom before homeroom commenced. Echoes of Principal Dembo's voice warned latecomers of consequences as they found their way, knowing this guy didn't play.

After watching the traffic, a delayed lightbulb finally lit. None of the student population looked like me. Most of the teachers and staff did not look like me. Stephen Decatur served the local Black population whose experiences did not help them embrace Caucasian interference too eagerly. Landlords, police, storeowners, and school administrators provided some of their only experiences with whites and many voiced negative opinions about their interactions, so they were leery. A few white men on staff taught in this Title One school to avoid being drafted and sent to Vietnam instead of a passion for children or education. A handful transformed into professional educators, but most professed they would leave the profession as soon as American troops exited Southeast Asia.

I was out of my element and clueless, without prior exposure, but willing to learn. Could I find acceptance? Would my efforts be embraced?

Feeling apprehensive because I had little to no communication with people of color, I reasoned that these students were simply kids in different packages. Unfortunately, many of these packages appeared disheveled, dressed in clothing that no longer fit, without basic school supplies like pencils or notebooks, dependent upon free or reduced lunches; the socio-economic poverty became evident to me. With hesitancy, I figured that I would give it a try and hope for good results. There, in what to me appeared a sea of hopelessness among these young people, I was forced to look beyond their impoverished exteriors, to forget the burdens and ignite the sparks. I would learn: to listen and observe better, to ignore preconceived notions, to acknowledge, to continually minimize and erase my implicit biases as I educated myself about a segment of the population with whom I had no previous contact or familiarity. Perhaps this place would teach me how to discover who students were, to instill hope and to search for their gifts. But I could assume nothing, start from square one, and do what I was paid to do, teach. Early on, I discovered that students from nurturing homes fared better and often filled seats in classes for higher achievers regardless of financial burdens. Others often raising themselves were armed with coping skills like savvy posturing or charades that hid their true insides, often empty and aching to be filled—something I would learn from their writings.

This dreamer would never be the same as my metamorphosis was to begin in that very building.

For the first few days, I observed various remedial reading classes in session. That meant no planning or teaching, just absorbing: learn the environment, watch the teacher/student interaction, take mental notes. There were no speech classes on the master board of student classes at the time, so my past courses and planning were irrelevant. The principal understood that my résumé was not a perfect fit, but his intention for me would be to fit in or sidetrack the system—something that happened often in at-risk labeled schools where staff could be grafted into emergency certification tracks. His goal included molding me into a reading teacher with the unwritten promise of developing some speech courses at a future time. (I knew not to hold my breath.) So, even though I offered minimal assistance and volunteered to help, I typically sat in the back of the room, strolled, browsed, or nodded, as I watched the dynamics for what seemed like an endless time.

For about seven days, I roamed from one teacher's classroom to another. I observed young and old, mostly females, each with unique techniques finding ways to read kids and maintain order. Some ruled with iron fists while others mothered and coddled…whatever worked but sometimes, nothing worked. "Repeaters", as they were labeled, spent class after class in the dean's office where reprimands threatened, and behavior modification methods were attempted. Discipline included some degree of corporal punishment, specifically paddling, which was legal at the time, occasional parent intervention, suspensions, and expulsion for extreme cases.

My adventure was unique. As I watched, I analyzed. Thinking I had the answer, the magic wand to work wonders, I waited with bated breath, excitement, and terror, for the day I could take control. It's easy to criticize when you're not on the stage. By week two, the opportunity arrived, but instant anxiety overwhelmed my body. My inner turmoil and fear of acceptance sparked a new daily ritual: I now vomited every June morning before I left home. It was an unexpected weight-loss program that I hoped would eventually end. The truth was I had lots to learn and no bag of tricks yet.

On Wednesday morning of the second week, I was unchained. Ms. Louise Latty, English chairperson, met me in the main office and handed me my first schedule, plus a list of her expectations: teach four sixth grade remedial reading classes, walk a dreaded hall patrol assignment, eat lunch, and use two free periods to observe or recover, whichever necessary.

"Deliver the lessons prepared by the absent teachers and maintain order," she directed, wearing her usual upside-down smile.

Ms. Latty permanently grimaced and never verbally encouraged me. Yet, her intimidating instruction and mentoring later helped me design a viable curriculum in a field where I was devoid of prior knowledge. On paper, my credentials looked terrific, but selling believability in front of middle schoolers was something else. At twenty-two, ripe for picking, I knew nothing about discipline or the reading curriculum. Heart palpitating with uncertainty and substitute filler lessons in hand, I jumped into the fire ready to be scorched. When the bell rang, I entered room 216.

Chapter 3

APPEARING DISENGAGED AND lethargic, they went through motions usually ignoring my suggestions to complete busy work assignments left by teachers who had closed up shop at this juncture. We managed to survive unbearable humidity, oppressive conditions. As I perspired profusely, I shifted before them wearing a washable dress that stuck to me and stocking that daily snagged and tore on the splintery desks. But I faced the challenge. Although the credo is to destroy substitutes in any way possible, thankfully, that did not occur. These youngsters just wanted out. Maybe they felt pity. They disregarded my instructions, ignored me, held private conversations, completed minimal paperwork later tossed on the front desk, and waited for the dismissal bell.

The routine continued all June. They were too hot and too tired to fight, which was a blessing in disguise. They weren't learning, but they weren't causing chaos either. I felt like a babysitter. My digestive track reminded me that I wasn't prepared for this setting, yet ironically, I survived those four brutal weeks and banked my weekly $200 checks, earning about $800 that long month, but it was over. Or so I thought.

During one of the final few days, Principal Dembo summoned me into his office and complimented my perseverance.

"Phillips, you made it. Here's a package for you, a full-time reading teacher, a $9400/year contract with full benefits and ten sick days beginning after Labor Day, September 1969."

Shoving a pen into my hands, he did not expect me to refuse. As I hesitated for seconds, I watch his eyebrow raise, his body language hint impatience, but he waited silently for my response. That day, I dared to sign my first official teaching contract! "Thank you, sir."

He nodded like I was wasting precious time. He snatched the agreement papers, and I placed the manila envelope filled with district policies, medical information, and a copy of my "I do" contract into my briefcase, left the building and headed home to share my employment news with my folks. Over the summer, I would run a drama program but now, I also intended to write an updated curriculum, as well as gain confidence during the two-month summer break. Otherwise, my G.I. tract would win my inner battle. I would not cede.

I think some teachers spend summers reenergizing, reflecting and rewriting plans while many others find secondary jobs. Bills still needed to be paid and with limiting salaries few in the profession had bulging pockets to handle financial responsibilities that continued during the summer. The outside world that thinks teachers are overpaid doesn't understand that the day never ends at final bell as perceived. Responsible teachers spend endless hours creating, tweaking, and correcting, a never-ending task, rather than just checking off work. Once one pile decreases, the next assignment is due, causing a cycle that continues for ten months. And forget the funds teachers spent to decorate and clean rooms to be more inviting. A few repainted walls and bought furniture to spruce up appearances. They had sprung for fans to help bear the heat. I did not understand those dynamics when I first entered the profession. My June adventure taught me many lessons.

Preparing for my first full year included hot-weather procrastination. After weekdays of completing my responsibilities directing creative dramatics at the theater day camp, why wouldn't I sunbathe at Jones Beach, a thirty-minute drive from home? I had a long-time boyfriend from college, socialized and placed school curriculum on the back burner thinking September might never arrive. But it did. Now, I was let loose with no mentors to direct me.

Chapter 4

THE HOT STICKY reminder of June returned, but this revitalized, eager teacher prepared to mold lives that morning before melting. Excited at first, I was teased with a schedule that read: Homeroom "SP". Honor students to begin my day. But after further perusal, to my dismay, my eyes scanned the page and I discovered that my schedule screamed of challenge. I greeted each day with top students only taking attendance before they scurried to accelerated classes. My class lists indicated names of students who frequented the detention room, mostly under-achievers, labeled emotionally unstable, struggling readers who never considered school anything more than a burden or a social setting where academic success was never a priority.

This was to be my destiny. After all, who else filled "remedial" classes? Colleagues informed me that as department newbie, I got their "rejects"—specific names that teachers refused to keep on their rosters because of prior experiences. Now those targeted kids were clumped together, all mine. The theory was better students were now freed of the interfering problem kids. They were repeaters, truants, discipline problems, the names that other veterans dreaded and refused to embrace. My challenge began as the opening bell reminded me to scurry back to dreary-looking room 216 where I would spend my year.

Hyperventilating, beads of sweat ran down my chest and back. Not a healthy sign. When facing extreme anxiety, my normally low blood pressure drops occasionally, causing me to faint. Skipping breakfast encouraged hypoglycemia issues as well, but I attempted to focus on the tasks at hand by listing details on the board: my name, the class section and welcoming news. Because I feared collapsing, I sipped orange juice as I practiced deep breathing and paced across the front of the room attempting to compose myself when the first student, a young boy, swaggered in.

It's difficult to describe the moment imprinted in my brain. Amid an inner-city Brooklyn school located in an area labeled disadvantaged, Title 1, I transformed. I began the day as a naïve, middle-class Jewish-American princess from Long Island, but I morphed into a more sensitive, intuitive, driven, young woman. This new journey commenced when I met Forrest, a twelve-year old "gangsta" who changed my world as I did his.

Chocolate-skinned, dressed in basic black, he exuded an aura of anger. He paused, stared, and assumed a challenging pose just a few feet from me. He was in my face! He was a beautiful child, almost perfect despite sunglasses hiding an eye that seemed to wander with his stare. (Later he shared the dastardly deed that resulted in that twisted eye muscle, scarring his handsome countenance.) He appeared older and was perhaps one of the hold-over non-achievers named on the infamous list of what some colleagues tagged, "kids who simply take up space!" (It's appalling to find no worth in a child.)

An "applejack" hat resembling a brimmed pancake sat cocked sideways on his head, stance antagonistic, and positioned uncomfortably in *my* physical space, he questioned in a churlish manner, "Who's the teacher?"

Without thinking of consequences, I blurted, "I am, and I know a gentleman takes his hat off in front of a lady!"

Not sure where that came from…*pause, breathe*, I told myself fearing my demise. Staring coldly, his massive black lashes blinked behind his shades, and I detected the slightest smirk, maybe just a lip quiver. He hesitated, removed his hat, moved about two feet in reverse, sat with arms folded in dead center, middle row, never taking his piercing, cold eyes off me. An endless silence, except for my pounding heart, dominated the room until others loudly barged in.

"TAKE YOUR HAT OFF, MAN! THERE'S A LADY IN FRONT OF THE ROOM!"

And so, it all began. Halting in their tracks, one by one, bold boys cowered and removed hats as they obeyed the directive from this mysterious young man. In silence, they marched toward seats as Forrest's powerful presence disciplined all in the room for me. His unsettling, almost stalking presence haunted me that period, but I steadily led the lesson, distributed the tasks for the period and observed only a slight mumble here and there as the crowd worked. Forrest and I occasionally made eye contact and with unspoken communication, he validated my position for all present. The intimidator threatened his peers but protected me. When the bell brought relief, bodies scurried to leave and collected the packet of work to evaluate the varying ability levels later that night. Forrest left last, handed me his paper, said nothing.

"Thank you, You're quite a leader."

He smirked and exited in silence. I did not realize that my immediate new bodyguard, Forrest, would be with me throughout my career, in my classes, in my stories, in my life.

No one dared misbehave in any of my classes, but it wasn't my own doing, no teaching wonder here. Forrest, the "hammer, an enforcer" nailed his classmates and eliminated any disorder. I didn't care because while they feared Forrest, they listened and learned, took baby steps. For the first week, those first five days went well. I coasted in every section because Forrest's power extended into every classroom. He ruled. I spent nights reviewing assignments, writing positive comments and constructive ideas to improve the work. If the year continued like this opening week, I would end my nervous stomach issue and might even make headway with the one hundred at-risk kids I served.

But at the time, truancy appealed to Forrest more than I did, so his days with me during my first contract year totaled eleven! Stories circulated amongst staff and filtered down to the new gal in town. Labeled incorrigible, this kid spent multiple weeks incarcerated in juvenile detention centers, and to everyone's surprise, behaved respectfully those eleven days in my class. I was warned not to get too comfortable around him, never to trust him. Colleagues scolded me, calling me naïve. Undoubtedly, he would rob me, key my car, or physically attack me if I didn't watch out! Skeptical, I heard them, discredited them, and ignored them. I communicated with Forrest and welcomed his presence the rare times he showed up.

Forrest was a conundrum, a volatile, complex preteen who softened whenever I neared. No one dared to cross him. Because of his reputation, he commanded a type of respect not only in school from peers but also, on the street. He strutted fearlessly and intimidated high schoolers near the Fulton Street subway, as well as adults who crossed his path. By age nine, he had been locked in detention centers eight times and did not fear consequences as he terrorized those he met.

I possessed unspoken permission to be part of his life. I patted his untouchable shoulder when I walked the aisle in class without a negative reaction. I almost embarrassed him when I complimented his handwriting, a work of art with all little letters the same size, a penmanship teaching guide. He scoffed and then ignored me. Occasionally, he scrutinized my corny remarks, shook his head in disbelief, but never challenged me to stop. When he removed his dark glasses, I complained it was too windy in the room whenever he batted those fan-like eyelashes. He dared not to smile, dared not react. That unsettling stare answered me, and for some reason, I understood it to be accepting. He was a haunting ghost that first year. When present, he said little, worked with no continuity, sporadically learning. Yet, his minimal work samples showed depth and promise. He could read and respond. If I could only unlock his trapped potential.

Even in his absence, because of him, I boldly walked around the building like Cain, untouched with a unique invisible mark on me. The word was out, and a hedge of protection surrounded me. I felt comfortable most of the time. My property, including my car, was safe as well. JHS 35 became a second home and although the year was an uphill battle and I was still in learning process mode, I became accepted and liked, and I liked back! Not too sure of what I was doing, I lured them with personal stories connected to the text and engaged my students little by little, making a minimal difference. They were buying in and developing trust. Perhaps they just feared Forrest's return from juvie and worked to avoid his wrath. Whatever the reason, I started to find strategies and pull a bit of magic out of my hat.

Attempting to be innovating, I introduced the "unbirthday party", an idea that later crashed before my eyes. Knowing that many students' birthdays passed without celebration, I decided a monthly sheet cake would ensure each child a special time, a tasty treat, a group party. To me, it was incomprehensible to ignore birthdays or let them pass without even a simple handshake of congratulations. Since teachers often spend their own funds on rewards and supplies, I knew on a first-year teacher's salary the undertaking dented my financial monthly budget, but I was determined birth dates needed to be acknowledged. I charted and displayed names monthly and observed their excitement over being acknowledged for something positive. Usually, we acknowledged the monthly celebrants, sang, and ate. That upbeat atmosphere prevailed for about four months and then, a battle erupted.

I hadn't read the mood fast enough or heard the provocative comments that sparked the chaos. Somebody "dissed" somebody else's mama and since mama comments were taboo, in an instant, the playful comments escalated, became accusations and fighting words. I was blind-sighted. Chocolate fudge cake flew across the room and an indescribable food fight mounted. This one was for REAL! Forget control. Forget birthday cakes. And of course, Forrest was absent, so I lost total control.

It took two threatening male hall patrol teachers shaking their heads at me to reestablish order. When decorum returned, I angrily announced the elimination of future parties from my routine. I realized that the class disciplinarian was not me. I needed Forrest!

Chapter 5

AS A NEW educator, I discovered that too many of my students never toured a museum or witnessed a live theater performance. Despite being just a few subway stops, a quick ride, many rarely left the neighborhood except during late August to shop for school clothes at discount street vendors on New York's Lower Eastside. Rarely visits to the Empire State Building, Statue of Liberty, a Broadway show or walk through Central Park were ever on family's "to do" lists. Families often could not provide opportunities to enjoy excursions out of the neighborhood because of financial concerns and/or work schedules. No visits to Little Italy or Chinatown where enticing aromas beckoned passers-by to taste the varied ethnic foods during street fairs or at local eateries that celebrate diversity. These were inconceivable ventures for too many of my students because they lacked an available adult to escort or the subway fare needed to travel. Thus, exposure to the world outside of Bedford Stuyvesant was usually non-existent. Inequities are maximized when students do not have an equal playing field because of a lack of experiences or exposure. This can create a void that affects student learning. For example, standardized tests often included reading passages about museum visits or vacation venues and without familiarity, a student may be unable to make necessary connections to the content of a text resulting in less understanding and poorer outcomes not based on actual student intelligence. That's where I entered the scene.

As the final months of my first full year approached, I decided to collaborate with colleagues, and we planned a school trip as a joint adventure. The goal: to escort our students on a guided tour of the Brooklyn Museum, followed by an informal picnic day in Prospect Park conveniently located across the street. We submitted the mandatory paperwork and received approval knowing that all transportation would be train travel because limited budgets never involved buses. After coordinating plans with other teachers, I distributed permission slips accompanied by a threatening lecture concerning expected behavior while on a trip.

"I'm not a babysitter and I'm not playing! You need to return the behavior contract signed by a parent or guardian by tomorrow. Also, I assigned buddies. If you're not happy, don't come. Questions?"

I distributed copies of both permission slips and the pairings. They complied. They loved leaving the school building with me, and leaving the building meant a day off in their eyes.

What a great way to end the school week with a Friday trip and the weather cooperating. Forest was no place to be found since that was his truancy year, so I did not expect him to participate. I questioned his whereabouts to no avail, but I was prepared to handle my responsibilities without him. With signed permission slips in hand, which I later learned were often forged, we abandoned the oppressive inside heat to explore a different section of the borough. At about 9:00 a.m., four classes of students and their teachers walked about three blocks to the nearby Fulton Street subway, hopped onto the A train, and switched to the Franklin Avenue Extension train to journey a couple of stops to our destination. Armed with special passes for free transportation and museum entry, students only needed to bring supplies. Most arrived with junk food, bottled drinks, and some change in their pockets while a few others carried blankets, bats, and balls. The cafeteria staff provided lunch for most, those with designated "free lunch" status and added a few extra sandwiches for needy or forgetful students who were unprepared.

The group's behavior on the train was satisfactory. Sure, they were a bit loud and excited, which was somewhat intimidating to others in the car traveling to downtown workplaces, but they created no disturbances. I sensed Forrest's absence and felt slightly unsettled but dismissed my uneasiness. *I can handle this*, I assured myself.

We arrived at about 9:40, knowing we needed extra time to gather and divide into smaller groups before our museum tour appointment at 10:00 a.m.

"It's so clean here!"

"Yup. No garbage."

"Well, I saw they got trash cans at the end of every street," one youngster remarked with surprise.

While waiting for the doors to open in the unfamiliar, more affluent area near the Park Slope neighborhood, they got a glimpse, a slight introduction to other worlds where streets were pristine and homes well-manicured. Naturally, the warnings and rules were reinforced as we lined up ready to enter the museum.

"NO PICNIC if you're out of order! Hands in pockets!" echoed from all four teachers.

We deposited our picnic belongings in a locked, protected area and then proceeded to follow designated tour guides in assigned groups with partners. Threats kept them in compliance as they rushed from one exhibit to the next, waiting for the afterparty. I suggested a "hands in pockets" policy to eliminate touching anything fragile and insisted the use of inside voices to avoid negative attention from onlookers. Some were enthralled by the gem exhibits, the large amethyst, opal, and emerald stones, but most skimmed and scanned, taking in the bare minimum preferring to whisper about the upcoming softball games. A few more ambitious learners took notes, knowing teachers would assign a written follow-up activity or reaction paper. I wondered what Forrest would be doing, who he would pal around with, what he might find interesting. Nervously, I watched my students during their first time as museum attendees!

Raised eyebrows and worried glances from museum escorts were unwarranted but expected when one hundred African American seventh graders congregate anywhere for a couple of hours. I think I held my breath; my eyes darted as I played watch guard until the tour ended. Guides also appeared relieved by the lack of negative incidents and more at ease as we bid thank you and farewell. Teachers nodded as we regrouped, gathered ourselves, and crossed Prospect Park West heading into the park. It was a bit before noon. We prearranged a two-hour window before the return trip would commence.

Brown paper bags ripped open, and food was vacuumed down within minutes before the games began. Some danced to tunes from transistor radios hidden in bookbags while others sat on blankets laughing. All appeared unburdened by the baggage they carried daily. A few took walks never wandering out of sight, but for the most part, softball games filled the open field area. Two male teachers joined the ballgame while I ran around with black garbage bags trying to keep the park as clean as when we arrived and then surveyed the overall scene since sports is not my thing. I counted heads again and again, knowing that twenty-five were in my charge. I felt accomplished. The sun smiled down upon us and the wind, which we never felt inside the cement school walls, blew so slightly that we knew it would be hard to pick up and leave when necessary.

One colleague, Mr. S, a young, hip math teacher, who chose being an educator rather than the soldier, blew the dreaded whistle signaling a fifteen-minute warning until departure. Sighing and complaining, they complied. Games ended, blankets folded, belongings gathered, final cleanup and headcount to follow. Despite moans and groans, our groups followed directions like little soldiers. If all went well, they dreamed of another excursion before the school year ended. Colleagues counted and gestured thumbs up.

And then, my turn: one short. I recounted: one student short! Heart pounding, I heard murmurs and immediately identified the missing culprit.

"VICTOR!"

Running through the other teachers' groups shouting, beckoning for Victor, my cries were unanswered. While time flew by, we all knew the rules. It was imperative to return before dismissal bell.

As the minutes rushed by, Mr. S and my other two colleagues approached me. "We've got to get back." They were sympathetic but decided to leave.

I watched seventy-five students march away as I stood frantic with my twenty–four. Perhaps I should have sent them home with my colleagues? I appeared distraught as I floundered, searching for a solution. Truth was, I did not know what to do. After what seemed an endless amount of time, a meek voice became an informant.

"Victor left with a few older boys who met him here."

I could not believe my ears, but the words rang true. Victor was often defiant, and I missed the warnings. I knew his disappearance would warrant consequences, but I had no solution. My mind raced. What would Forrest do? He'd probably have told me not to let Victor come. Keep the problems back in the building, but I missed the signs. Beads of sweat formed, and I felt nauseous as I paced, trying to find a way out of this mess. Although my kids tried to calm me down, I stood scrambling for an answer surrounded by twenty-four bodies. I tried to stay composed but was ready to cry.

"There he is!" someone shouted. "Victor, get the fuck over here! Sorry, Miss."

After about twenty minutes of chaos, Victor simply reappeared with his "boys" like nothing happened. I wanted to wring his neck and he knew it.

"Are you kidding me? You've got everybody worried and waiting!" I shouted.

I was so irate I didn't even ask him if he was okay. I learned he was just fine and defiant.

"I'm not going back with you guys. I'm staying with my boys and got a subway token, so you can leave without me," he informed me rudely.

I was flawed, to say the least. Despite my protests, threats and raised volume, he ignored my pleas and was suddenly gone again. I was at a loss. Internally, I screamed, my heart was pounding, and I ceded. "Let's go. We're late."

I marched toward the station in silence and within seconds, we boarded the train. Twenty minutes later, I returned my class minus one to the school building a bit after three. The school's student body was already dismissed and since the students all lived in the area, they walked home carefree.

"Don't worry Miss. It's not your fault. It'll be okay," a student patted my shoulder.

"We got your back. Victor's an ass."

"Too bad you didn't bring Forrest. He would've kicked some ass," another chimed.

Despite the kind words, I was overwhelmed and in tears. I stood in a basically abandoned building and felt like a hopeless wreck. Most faculty members and office workers fled on Fridays immediately after the dismissal bell to enjoy a weekend and I had no clue what procedures to follow.

Looking back, I knew to just call Victor's home and report his defiance. Without cell phones or computers at the time, I needed to find his contact information and get to his parent, but I was in shock. I was a novice, the newbie, and stupidly I did not help myself. While retrieving my belongings, head spinning, ready to leave, I noticed an office room door ajar. Thank goodness! The dean of students still sat in his office. He wasn't working, just "chillin'" sipping from a pint, after school hours, winding down from the hassles that accompany a week's end.

Ranting, I frantically explained my dilemma without taking a breath and waited for the advice that would eradicate my anxiety.

"Pray baby…"

That's what he offered. With a pit in my stomach, I gathered my things, got into my little red car, blasted the music, and attempted to erase my memory. (Obviously, this vivid experience never left me.) Why didn't I just call his mother? How foolish! I neglected to cover my ass even after I returned to the school. Inexperience took control and I escaped to enjoy my weekend and tried to forget the worry even though it nagged at me.

Little could I imagine what Monday would bring.

I spent Sunday tweaking my lesson plans and repressed worrying about the debacle that could ruin my career. Monday arrived. Maybe I succumbed to a temporary brain freeze, but I forgot about what could be awaiting me—the consequences of my inaction. Early morning, while teaching my students during second period, a voice blared through the loudspeaker interrupting my delivery. "Ms. Phillips to the office NOW!"

Summoned to the main office, I faced a firing squad: principal, vice principal, English chairperson and a mature-looking stranger who happened to hold the title of school board president. Mrs. M. stood dead center and hidden slightly behind her was her son Victor, the missing culprit from my field trip roster.

My world turned upside down, inside out, when first this lady laced into me for leaving Victor in the park until 8:00 p.m. She was shouting and breathing down my neck, chastising me for not contacting her or an administrator. Her volume reached a crescendo. Then silence as she expected a response. My eyes welled. "I am so sorry."

I was meekly apologizing until I noticed the smirk on Victor's face. Something clicked. Somehow, I summoned the courage to describe his behavior, to tell her exactly what he did and to describe his defiance. "But I did not desert your son. He decided to leave his assigned buddies and go off with two older boys he recognized in the park. Then, he returned late to inform me that he was not returning with the class. Before I could persuade or even threaten him about his actions, he turned and left. I waited twenty minutes extra for him with twenty-four of his classmates."

I spewed the details with clarity, described his attitude and his company. I made certain she knew that although I was wrong, her son was no victim, no angel. I never reported that I sought out the dean before leaving school because he offered no guidance. Never gave him up.

With raised brows, Mrs. M.'s head twisted back and forth towards her son, trying to validate whether my words rang true. His body language signaled his typical behavior and before he uttered a word, she wound up, hauled off and slapped him across his face with a blow that nearly knocked him to the floor. After what seemed like endless silence, she turned to me, accusatory pointer finger in my face. "That doesn't mean what you did was right!"

With that, she stormed out of the room with Victor close behind, wearing her reddish handprint across his cheek. My chairperson pursued her, had her ear, assuring her that repercussions would follow my poor judgment.

Crying and dramatic, in crisis mode, I volunteered to resign. "Do you want me to leave?" I sobbed.

Behind those closed doors, my principal upbraided me for my ridiculous ignorance of rules but brushed away the idea of me leaving the job. By the end of that day, the consequences were determined: a copy of the letter placed into my file appeared in my mailbox. Because of my irresponsibility, I was restricted from taking part in any field trips for the remainder of the school year. *Whew!*

Thank goodness it was late spring. After a couple of months' punishment, the appalling experience would be behind me, and my career could continue. It took time to rebuild my confidence but two years later, I organized successful field trips never forgetting my first and never letting my guard down again.

Chapter 6

ADMINISTRATORS REALIZED THAT a unique bond grew between Forrest and me, so they collaborated and devised a trial plan for the following September: Assigning him to both my homeroom and scheduling double reading classes with me could foster this positive relationship, keep him closer to me and away from any staff members that he antagonized. Hopefully, this might minimize his poor attendance pattern. The goal: keep him in school but out of the Dean's office, a place he frequented for paddling when his behavior could not be tolerated. Corporal punishment was condoned. Students opted for typically three smacks with a three-inch thick perforated wooden paddle heaved without mercy by a discipline dean, whose behavior modeled one suffering from a Napoleonic complex. For most in trouble, even the macho teens, the spankings hindered their ability to sit when they returned to class. When students weighed the consequences of phone calls home and parent involvement versus a quick physical punishment, they overwhelmingly chose the latter.

"Don't be calling my mom. Her whippings are worse!"

"My dad will kill me if you bother him about some bullshit. He'll take his stick to my sorry ass."

"If my grandma answers the phone and hears it's the school, I can never go home."

Busy parents and guardians did not welcome school administrators burdening them at work or home, and their children knew the repercussions of parent involvement were far worse than a few stings.

Forrest was so used to punishment that he developed a hardened shell and perhaps calloused rear, never flinching from the paddle's sting to the dismay of the inflictor. As a final intervention before sending him to some residential setting again, administrators took a chance on me, yes, because of our positive school bonding but mainly because they ran out of alternatives. Forrest, a repeater at Spofford Juvenile Detention Center, a lock-up historically plagued with fights and abuse designed to reform troubled youth, never feared the juvie placement. Lock-up increased his resentment. He devised coping mechanisms to avoid becoming a target for other inmates when incarcerated. He acted crazed and unpredictable, sang in his cell all night just for spite and rather than back down, he morphed into an aggressor.

"I didn't give a shit," he later shared. "I sang so loud and all night long that they kept threatening to shut me up for good, but I beat them at their game. Nobody bothered me. I just did what I had to until I got sprung or until the judge threatened me again."

Although Forrest was small in stature, they feared him or labeled him psycho. Peers avoided contact and his style saved him both in lock-up and on the streets. Back in the community, in desperation, school administrators gambled, attempting to alter Forrest's attitude and if not, frankly, get him off their hands. If our partnership failed, they would find a reason for expulsion, be rid of him permanently and toss him to a different school. But they gambled one last time. The only glitch was holding him back from seventh grade.

When Forrest first discovered that he would repeat grade six, I thought he would tear the place apart.

"That's crap! Gonna leave me back? I gotta sit with these knuckleheads when I know more than all of them? I'm outta here! Hate this place."

Grabbing his arm, I explained that his 6H5 class placement included me for most of the day and like magic, his attitude changed. His confrontational style seized. Outwardly he offered little reaction, little resistance, but his presence was felt. In fact, his shock and anger of not being socially promoted soon faded. The class H5 label signified lower achievers, a tag he would normally find offensive, but after his initial outburst, he did not object. He filled his chair. He was there; with other than one glitch of about a two-week period when I thought he reverted to his old style, he was there—from truancy to a year of almost perfect attendance! After the previous year's record of a mere eleven days in school, a transformation occurred. Even when sick, he never missed a day. Never tardy, never disruptive, consistently quiet, sitting and completing assignments, a new Forrest appeared and blended into the group though I knew he was different. The transformation shocked all of us. Daily, I prayed that his grenade pin never dislodged. The experiment appeared successful. Administrators' insight was correct as our pairing seemed to be a new beginning for both of us. Trust and friendship melted his frozen exterior and warmed my heart.

Although age might distort some of my recollections, there was that one incident that angered him enough to take a school break. It was no longer the norm for him to be absent and with no home phone, the mystery remained for a bit, about two weeks. I figured his cooldown took time and he would get back on schedule. I was right.

He arrived and said little. I wondered about his hiatus but did not question or act surprised. I just let him be. He complied all period, completed his work and then after the bell sounded and the group left the room, he walked towards my desk and shoved a box of chocolate-covered cherries into my hands.

"Here." He scooted away.

I knew to accept his peace offering without question. He rarely smiled, but he no longer brooded. He batted those long eyelashes, passed the candy and without missing a beat, left the class not looking back as I shouted, "Missed you. Thank you!"

Months later, he pushed an unwrapped ring with tiger's eye center stone into my palm and when I hesitated, the fire in his eyes ignited. I dared not question him at the time, thought twice and graciously accepted the offering. I slipped it on to my finger and he nodded in approval. I wore it proudly even though it was probably stolen merchandise. These secret gifts became gestures that solidified his loyalty. At the time, I was unaware that he also initiated his private, protective plan to assure my safety both in the building and its surrounding hood.

His class section was filled with many of his cronies, other holdovers, as well as a few younger members of the local Hellcats, a gang that ravaged the neighborhood intimidating, stealing, and spreading fear. My pupils, led by the lucky, inexperienced young teacher whose room became a "dumping ground" where those labeled least likely to succeed, filled the seats whenever their attention spans allowed them to do so. Isolated, they were manageable but all in one setting seemed impossible. Some bobbed up and down especially when they refused to take their daily doses of Ritalin, the anti-anxiety drug of choice at the time.

My head spun when I realized that the roster contained too many non-performing kids who most faculty tossed from class, gave up on the year before and refused to pass another year with the culprits threatening to quit if they appeared on a roster. Now, the whole bunch sat in my room. I waited for any one of them to explode at any time. But because Forrest modeled perfect behavior and shot disapproving glances towards an "acting out" buddy, he calmed any impending storm. Despite some hurdles, the group congealed and worked together.

Because of my relationship with Forrest, my reputation grew. I became known as the teacher who dealt effectively with "dysfunction". At the time, none in the group were labeled "special needs" or had accompanying IEP (individual education plans), but the unwritten label spread: emotionally handicapped, the known misfits, almost the entire bunch.

With complicated lives, initially few succeeded with reading assignments, almost no one completed homework, but at least they all behaved. Manners were free and I thought I might threaten to teach them after school, but that was never necessary. I smiled, nodded approval, and acted personally hurt when someone disobeyed. I patted and hugged because it was permitted in the 70s, and these kids needed positive reinforcement. You see, I had Forrest and with him, my group fared well and often made me proud. At first, I thought I had a special gift and eventually I did discover my hidden talents, but at that time, student management was not my forte. It was orderly in my room because Forrest ruled, not me. His threatening reputation permeated all sections I taught, whether he was present or not, which made my job easier.

Chapter 7

EVERY TUESDAY MORNING, the daily schedule modified to include a special assembly. We marched into the auditorium, in unison sang the Black anthem, "Lift Every Voice", and sat as audience for various programs. Usually, kids cooperated because the entertainment removed them from the drudgery of classroom work for an hour or so. Guest speakers, entertainers, a few athletes, and motivators attempted to reach anyone in the crowd, but the musical programs engaged them best. Talent permeated the student population so when a preteen volunteered to sing or dance, we felt beamed to the Apollo for a special treat.

I discovered that administration ran a weekly contest challenging classes to dress up for assembly: boys and girls in white-collared shirts and dark pants or skirts. Unfortunately, most of my kids who could care less about a silly contest, couldn't afford another outfit, and white was never the first option during shopping for necessities. Yet, I noticed that they thrived when rewarded.

I wanted my "leper" group that others avoided to be recognized in some way. I had to change or at least enhance their image. I loved to shop. At home, my family members gave me assignments to find a product for my mom or sister and it became a personal challenge, a game to get the right item for the best bargain price. Driven, I elected a weekend shopping spree at a discount department store, Alexander's, where I purchased two dozen white shirts and blouses in assorted sizes and styles, hung them like soldiers in the classroom's back closet and secretly prepared for the following week. Like an excited child full of secrets and exploding with enthusiasm, it was imperative to get Forrest on board to support my efforts.

"I went shopping," I said enthusiastically. "Look at what I got! "I pointed towards the closet. "Now we can win the assembly contest! Pick a shirt and let's go for it!" Hoping he would comply, I grabbed his hand and walked towards the new merchandise.

"You're whack."

To him I sounded so dorky, but my eyes pleaded. Without saying a word, groaning under his breath, he begrudgingly heeded to my wishes. He sifted through the choices and selected a shirt. His action, strictly to only make me happy, led by example. Well, it wasn't example. As students sauntered in, he commanded the troop. "Get a shirt."

Some stopped in their tracks.

"You heard me, get a shirt!"

He ordered and directed his peers towards the closet to find a shirt that worked. They never questioned, but their quizzical expressions warranted his response.

"We're dressing for the assembly." One sentence. The Pied Piper spoke, all listened and obeyed. Perfectly attired, we headed for the auditorium, many with their heads bowed in embarrassment. The room packed quickly, so when we entered, faces stared. We looked like a church choir something rarely seen in 35. We shut the humming down when our shocked Principal Dembo addressed the group and announced: "Miss Phillips and class 6H5, please stand! One hundred percent assembly dress!" He sparked the clapping,

As winners, this beaming teacher and her group of leftovers stood to be recognized in uniform dress code! Although the kids appeared mortified and reluctant to be labeled goody goodies, they accepted the applause and the prize, then shrunk into their chairs covering faces, hoping to disappear. Later during lunch, they giggled as they gobbled the pizza reward since food always worked as reinforcement and filled some hungry tummies and souls. They made my day. I vowed to win again and again.

"Next week, we will do it again," I cheered.

Many groaned, but no one objected. I washed and ironed those cotton shirts as needed and until threadbare because every week, we dressed to impress, the Forrest/Phillips ritual. I framed the earned certificates and hung them on newly decorated room 216 walls. I was grateful, and my hero knew it.

Chapter 8

TIMES WERE DIFFERENT. Teachers met with students and shared extracurricular activities both after school and on weekends. We weren't afraid to give rides or spend time alone with our kids. In some ways, we were naïve and in others, maybe it was safer back then and our intentions were never questioned. Without exposure to the outside world, my students knew only their "hood", a more downtrodden area where socioeconomics impacted lives and despair was the norm. Hard-working women struggled to feed families while a sea of disheartened men could not find gainful employment. With sporadic work schedules, many hid frustrations, sitting together on stoops endless mornings outwardly joking but inwardly hoping lives could change. Unfortunately for some, drugs and alcohol permeated the area and became the medicine that healed wounds. And too many children suffered. Often raising themselves and younger siblings, they grew up fast without carefree childhood adventures or quality family time. They knew the streets and learned how to avoid becoming victimized. There were rarely any dinner table conversations, no exposure to museums, no vacations. Only at the onset of the school year did I witness students clad in new shoes or clothing those first few days when they celebrated the purchases, but there were no future shopping sprees. On the contrary, many coped with bare cupboards, cold quarters, erratic space heaters, absentee landlords, cardboard cutout linings in worn-out shoes, army/

navy store used jackets that substituted for winter coats. And weekly visits to local laundromats topped the chore list since no washer/dryers were in apartments. Too many led latchkey lives, even the little ones.

At the time, Forrest did not share his plight, but I sensed the urgency to intervene. He was a gypsy boy, finding whatever he needed in the streets. On Saturdays, I drove back to Bed-Stuy, picked him up in front of his home around ten and filled his day. I insisted his belly be full as we shared real New York pizza and root beer floats or cold cuts covered in mayo piled onto Kaiser rolls. These were new treats accompanied with exploration trips for him. I introduced him to museums, frequented bowling alleys, explained movies, ran around in Flushing Meadow Park, or let him join a local basketball game. We attended Broadway shows, with his favorite being the musical, "The Me Nobody Knows". But the weekend fantasies ended when at sunset I returned "Cinderfella" to what I thought was his gated brownstone home. In time, I discovered this drop-off spot substituted for the project apartment he shared with his older sister and her children, a spot he reluctantly left to sleep in the hallway. He never revealed his true living conditions until much later in life, but I was aware that Forrest, a survivor bound to gang life, lived day to day, relying only on himself to get by.

The more time we spent together, the more I absorbed. He continued to school me in the art of survival and "hipped" me to the issues and lifestyles of those in my classroom. I recall acting as beauty consultant, advising one girl to limit the Vaseline she slathered over her skin in what I believed an effort to prevent an "ashy" appearance. I often witnessed the young girls applying lotions to remedy dry skin issues, so I assumed. Forrest tugged at my arm, pulled me aside and interrupted my intervention in hopes of saving me from embarrassment.

"She's getting ready for a fight. That's what you do. You grease up so nobody can leave scars. I know cause she's got her hair ready."

Her hair, corn-rowed to the scalp, was styled for damage control. Enemies could not create bald spots by grabbing handfuls of hair—not possible with this type of braiding. After I gulped and digested that information, he cautioned me to be aware of possible personal injury.

"Ya need to learn. It's bad out here. Ya know you always wear those earrings. They're too big. Somebody can stick their fingers in those hoops and just pull."

He warned me about ripped earlobes, and I winced when given too much information, though much of it came in handy.

I acquired additional lessons in travel as well. I alternated between driving my beetle car and boarding the train from my new Queens apartment. I could take the number 7 train in Flushing and then transfer to take the A train to school. When Forrest discovered this, he found it imperative to instruct me in the art of subway riding.

"Stand with your back against a wall or door but be careful when it opens. Check out the crowd but don't stare! You don't know who's carrying or whose face is on some wanted poster in the post office. You've seen them, right?"

I nodded. Then he added rules:

- Never stand alone at a pole with others around you who could bump you or poke you cause you're cute. Unless you got an umbrella to whack with.

- If you sit, don't leave your pocketbook on your lap or just over your arm to grab. Hook it around your head so it's harder to grab. But give it up if you gotta. Ain't worth your life.

- Sit nearer to an exit so you can get off if you must.

- Don't be walking country-like.

- Oh, and get some pepper spray. Better yet, I can get you mace.

With new protective mode in place, I was paranoid, but I avoided victimization when traveling on the local A and F trains. My pocketbook never rested on one shoulder; it draped across my chest making its disappearance less likely. I learned to walk with a minimal swagger and postured with enough style to avoid becoming a target. It grew easier during the four-block walk from the Fulton Street station to the Decatur and McDonough school location because Forrest spread the word. I was not to be touched! His invisible veil of protection followed my path, and my walk was uneventful. That was all I needed. I never got mace and I never had to use my trusty pepper spray. And when I parked for work, strict rules went into effect, Forrest style.

"Stay off those small side streets. You stay on Decatur or McDonough. Ride around and wait for a spot if you have to. We watch your car anyway."

Prohibited from using side streets and constrained to specific spots, Forrest or his friends could watch my car more easily. Frequent burglaries and vandalism left teachers' rides without batteries, radios, eight-track tape changers and with added key scratches and/or dents left in retaliation of unresolved school conflicts. Armed with new street smarts, I moved freely through the school building and surrounding neighborhood.

I might look different from others in the community, but I became a known regular and community members nodded approval when I frequented a local McDonald's or grocery store. While I absorbed unique lessons in survival from him, Forrest learned trust and loyalty.

In my Flushing apartment, he noticed my every move. When I needed extra pizza cash, I hid funds in a Band Aid box in my medicine cabinet. Shaking his head in disbelief, he removed the bills. "Naw, this ain't happening."

He transferred the money to a less likely place of discovery, insisting that any savvy thief could find my few twenties. When we shopped, he whisked grocery bags from my arms, refusing to let me carry anything even when he appeared burdened by their heaviness. He held the umbrella, opened car doors, and surveyed every destination in Queens like an adult protective services agent. And when my neighbors winced at the alien Black boy invading the primarily white residency of their building, Forrest drilled them with either his cold eyes or his ice face until I calmed him down. With me, he ventured into a foreign world where people of color rarely existed, slowly integrating the area leaving neighbors still leery of their recent entry into upper-middle-class apartment dwellings. At the time, the only diversity evident in my high-rise apartment were a few Asian families who moved to Queens and ran local eateries.

To the outside world, we were an unlikely duo, but we meshed and triumphed despite the stares and opposition of the era.

Chapter 9

EARLY DECEMBER, FORREST developed an air of secrecy and disappeared more frequently during the school day. His morning pre-class time visits were less frequent and afternoon talks became sporadic. His periodic check-in during class changes minimized and although I was curious about the change, I supposed his time was being divided between friends and the street. Maybe it was the beginning of a healthy readjustment, a separation and integration into typical student behaviors. Still, I heard no reports of mischief, so all seemed copacetic.

Before long, I discovered his whereabouts in an unfortunate incident that tested our unity. He had spent endless hours before classes, during study periods and after school in the ceramics art room where he ambitiously labored to create a bowl, an original, a Christmas present designed and molded for me. Because of his positive transformation, Forrest was permitted extra time to complete his project with the Ceramics teacher before the upcoming holiday break arrived. Since Forrest usually made life uncomfortable for many teachers, his presence and enthusiasm were initially a refreshing change. Until the crisis!

Unfortunately, the teacher placed the original creation into the kiln prematurely before it had dried or before the oven was at the correct temperature. *Poof!* The bowl exploded into slivers and bedlam erupted.

As Forrest's rage soared in the art room, errand boys hustled to find me. The intercom blared into from the speaker my room. "Miss Phillips, get to the ceramics room NOW!"

The assistant principal summoned me to intervene and to save the art room from total calamity. Without hesitation, I left my post and scurried toward the chaos. When I opened the door, Forrest was raging and threatening the teacher. "You fucked it up! I could kill your sorry ass!"

I discovered that the teacher, in an attempt to appease Forrest, donated a peace offering, an ashtray he designed trimmed with zodiac signs to replace the broken mess sitting inside the kiln, but his suggestion exacerbated the frustrated new artist. Forrest's hours of toil were irreplaceable, and this substitution was rejected. He was hysterical.

Although Forrest was no match for the older, six-foot tall, burly teacher in control, he was ready for combat never thinking about his sizeable opponent or the consequence of his actions. He clenched a broken slice of the shattered bowl as he stalked the teacher. Spontaneous combustion. That was what I witnessed! Fury raged. Forrest appeared irrational and wild. Seconds after assessing his behavior, I slithered towards my friend whose actions resembled that of an uncaged, desperate rabid animal. In a calm, monotone voice, I attempted to redirect his energy like a hostage negotiator talking down an enemy and quelling the fire, continually whispering, "Forrest please, Forrest please. Forrest, I'm here. Let it be."

After what felt like an eternity, something clicked, his erratic movements and his fuming lessened. Other administrators ready to grab him stopped as I directed them further away. They restrained themselves, removed the teacher, breathed sighs of relief and backed out of the room as the crisis ended.

Just the two of us left. Now refocused, Forrest dropped a jagged piece of his fractured project from his hand and together, we transferred slivers and chunks of the bowl from the cooled kiln into the industrial-sized waste can. The storm was over. Ironically there were no consequences, no punishment; no one was harmed.

Unfortunately, the art therapy terminated, and Forrest eased back into old routines. He continued to attend school, often as my appendage rather than attending classes. No one objected. Christmas came and passed, the New Year began and before I knew it, the winter passed without further incidents.

Chapter 10

ONE FRIDAY AS spring approached, I took the subway to work aware that my sister arranged to pick me up and together, we would venture out to Lakewood, New Jersey, where my parents relocated and downsized to a small condominium close to my mom's niece. There, we either shared an uncomfortable pull-out bed or I lined pillows across the living room floor and bedded down. Either way, it was a journey of love with poor accommodations. My folks left Long Island, moved shortly after a devastating stroke impacted my father's life and stole the daddy I once knew. Paralyzing the right side of his body and causing aphasic speech, his disabilities impacted his ability to ever work again. My folks sold the Valley Stream home and moved to New Jersey to live in a more affordable community of senior citizens, slowing financial concerns and life's pace for dad who never regained what he lost.

The school day ended at three, but I invited Max, who knew of my teaching passion, to join my classroom and witness me in action. I suggested that she arrive earlier afternoon so she could time with my kids. Expected at one and always on time, I peered out the window and spotted her parked 1971 Plymouth Scamp, but no sign of Max. I knew no one else dared to own that car because of its color. It was labeled "curious yellow", made only that year, a paint color never to be poured again. It resembled the yellow banana in the Curious George books, so I assume that is how manufacturers labeled the paint. During the daylight hours, it appeared to be shockingly iridescent and in cloudy or rainy weather, it somehow turned putrid chartreuse. She had unmistakably arrived, but where was she?

After what seemed like too long a time to check in at the main office and climb one staircase to the second floor, I left the room unattended to find her. As I approached the staircase, I noticed her standing frozen in place with two of my renegades blocking her path.

"Are you messin' with my blood?" I snapped.

"Sorry miss. We don't do anything, just checking her out."

They claimed everything was cool and scampering away, denied any attempt to take her gold chain, a possession she proudly wore around her neck. I assured my shaken baby sis that all was well, no harm would come to her…just a typical tactic used with strangers. That was Max's introduction to my home away from home in Bedford Stuyvesant. Her first-hand recollection as an outsider reinforced the image: a risky environment that screamed, "Outsiders, beware! Know your place!"

Although I remained teaching in JHS 35 for ten years. she dared not visit again after that one encounter. But this was now my home, and exposure to difference changed my vision. I was not an outsider. I was right where I belonged.

I ventured beyond the school walls during the following school year once the ban on school trips was lifted. In May, a few fellow teachers and I scheduled a trip to New York City to tour around the island of Manhattan on the Circle Line Boat. We negotiated a group fare rate that was doable if we spent most of the year having students pay for the trip. Students could manage small weekly contributions and by adding a bit of teachers' personal funds, the trip could be fully funded. We started collecting weekly contributions from the students and had enough to schedule the early May sailing. We brought boxed lunches provided at no charge by the school since the majority of our population still qualified for the free lunch program. Again, most carried pocket change to purchase drinks, snacks, or a possible souvenir during the voyage. With signed permission slips and cooperative weather, about one hundred kids and four teachers embarked on a water discovery journey although too many of the kids had minimal exposure to pools or beaches and feared the water.

In reality, here were students from all five New York boroughs on the boat who jostled for positions near the railings to watch departure. Although we expected a cooler day in early May, the sun broiled us, and relief would only arrive when the boat's movement stimulated a breeze. My students laughed at my overuse of sunscreen, sunglasses, and sun hat, teasing me about my pale complexion to their browner skins.

"You're like these white folks who wanna be brown. I see them silly ladies all the time," Forrest laughed and rolled his eyes at me.

I shot him a look, which he acknowledged as a "don't go there" message. I knew from prior experiences that I could turn tomato red if I did not use sunscreen.

"I think I'll go look at the ladies," he quipped and turned to join his peers.

Although the sun was intense, the breeze stimulated by the boat's movement brought relief from the unnaturally warm, muggy weather. The kids with assigned buddies wandered freely around the boat with most groups sticking together, but some, including Forrest, intermingled with outsiders their age from different schools. Harmless adolescent flirtations sparked as they giggled and stared at strangers they found attractive. I witnessed healthy conversations as youngsters crossed cultures with one another while others surveyed the geography around them. Some stood by railings the entire time, pointing out landmarks and reveling in the wind off the waterway, knowing that it was short-lived since in the hood, buildings blocked these refreshing elements from their streets. Others purchased ice cream from the onboard concession stand, licking frantically as it melted in the heat.

All was wonderful until a whistle signaled docking time and headed towards the pier. I gave the kids a heads up letting them know that it was about that time to depart for our subway trip back to Brooklyn and the school.

A little before the boat arrived, two teachers from a different school in a more affluent neighborhood cornered me. "Your kids threatened some of ours, demanding money!" one stated in an accusatory manner. They insisted that a bunch of my boys terrorized theirs and extorted money from them.

"Excuse me?" I remarked quizzically. "I'll get to the bottom of this."

Appalled, I began a round-up and started to question my kids. I guess I initially assumed the accusation credible, believing her kids must have been victimized by my savvy inner-city bunch. Shame on me! But I did what was necessary. First, I interrogated my group who swore innocence and frankly their stories were believable and made more sense.

"Miss, they're lying. All we did was talk," they nodded in agreement.

"Ya see that. They see some *niggas* and here we go again. Do you actually think I'd let them do this to you?" Forrest was fuming.

I second-guessed myself, but knew I had to get to the bottom of this before we docked. I listened to onlookers, passengers who came to my students' defense. They had watched the youths at play and witnessed simple excitement and no signs of intimidation. After intense questioning to resolve the issue, I discovered that the accusers whose lack of exposure to diversity kept them frightened, apparently felt uncomfortable around unfamiliar Black kids whose high energy and excitement intimidated them.

"Before you assume, get your facts separated from your lies," I said.

I confronted the accusers and embarrassed them for biased fabrications and their students' blatant lies. Rather than admit that they enjoyed conversations with Black youth, they covered up their interest with a made-up story. Eventually, their teachers conceded that probably nothing had occurred, so no harm-no foul. They took no blame for the chaos they caused, walked away and all were cool except for me. With a heightened awareness of racism, I experienced yet another lesson regarding the obstacles faced by my students.

"Hey miss, now you know." Forrest pointed to his skin.

I didn't live inside their skin and easily underestimated the depth of their hurt. I felt that my own implicit bias also may have surfaced when I questioned my kids even if only for minutes. This was yet another unfortunate introduction to racial profiling and reality checks.

Something terrible had taken place: my students of color were stereotyped, frightened, and ultimately angered and saddened by the fabricated accusations. Later the kids laughed, hid their angst by claiming that white kids found all Black kids scary.

"Just another day. Glad they didn't call the cops on us!" Forrest added.

Many seemed to let the ignorant assumption roll off their backs, but for some who remained quiet, I think the pain ran deep.

On a lighter note, I challenged Forrest often in the classroom. I remember the day newly purchased reading equipment, the latest panacea to the world's reading problems, were unveiled. Unique machines each designed for a specific purpose would focus on different reading concerns hindering a variety of students. Some flashed vocabulary sight words that needed to be memorized for basic understanding. A second set of machines was called *controlled readers*. Their primary purpose was to train the eye to move left to right, to read a story without digressing. Machine speed increased with reading fluency and individualized pacing. While students peered into the machine window designed much like ophthalmology equipment to focus on a story, they could alter the speed of a moving light that highlighted words as it moved right. This personalized instruction allowed students to adjust pacing as needed, so the more at-risk could slow the pace while the accelerated student could quicken it. When vocabulary became more challenging, pace could be adjusted to help students who needed time to understand meaning of new words in context. After completing a section, written responses to questions assessed comprehension on literal levels, as well as higher order competencies.

Motivated by the novelty of the project and the possession of new equipment, students worked individually using different equipment and after completing a section successfully they moved on. I rotated around the room monitoring progress. Yet, when I checked on Forrest, I stopped in my tracks.

"What exactly are you supposed to be doing?"

I chastised him for fooling around when I noticed the machine's light speed was set at maximum level and the pace moved too quickly for his eyes to follow.

"Are you kidding me?" There was no way a boy handicapped with a vision problem, with an eye muscle too weak to focus, could work at the setting on his machine. "Are you purposely wasting time? Forrest, you're killing me."

"You don't believe I'm done? I finished this silly work already," he claimed defiantly.

"I'm tryin to move ahead and get to the next dumb story."

Suspicious and determined to catch him lying, I was up for a challenge. Without a word, I thrusted the corresponding question sheet into his hands, daring him to prove his proclaimed ability. He glared, said nothing, sat down and went to work finishing quickly.

"Are you happy now? Told you I was done with this crap. You really piss me off," he mumbled under his breath, glared in my direction, and stormed out of the room needing to cool down. No one looked up, moved a muscle, or uttered a word. They sat at their machines in silence awed by the first confrontation they witnessed between us.

Of course, I stood dumbfounded and embarrassed when his reading prowess earned him a perfect score on the story's comprehension review. Like a puppy, I cowered a bit as he won the contest, and I went after him, but he was nowhere in sight.

Forrest earned his smug attitude. Misplaced in a remedial class, he would never be transferred to the honors program where he belonged because, emotionally, he needed to stay with me and benefit from the nurturing offered in my setting. But he was so annoyed with me over the reading machine incident that he took a short hiatus from school and missed a bunch of school days. I was afraid he had walked out permanently, but about ten days later he returned. Ours was the first relationship he trusted and that trumped his anger. I could have lost that trust when I questioned him, but the bond was stronger than the temporary feud.

I just learned to "differentiate" instruction before the label became vogue thirty years later. I decided to supply Forrest with more innovative program readings and higher-order thinking questions. I used whatever I had in a room with limited resources and created inferential questions of my own as an extension to what was provided. When necessary, I bought suitable material to supplement work. I discovered early in my career that many teachers dug into their own pockets when the school cupboards were bare.

Nothing much is innovative in teaching; theories get overhauled, renamed, retried. In the 70s, individualized instruction was the buzz term. No matter how homogeneous the class population, teachers were to focus on students' individual growth plans adjusting them to meet their personal needs at the time. In 2010, it was differentiation—regardless of class composition, lessons needed to be differentiated and adjusted to the learning styles and needs of each student; practically the same theory, new descriptive terms. The only change in education of epic proportion arrived with the influx of technology that offers instant communication and research to those who are technologically savvy and possess the equipment necessary for success, something that varies along socio-economic lines. I believe it is still difficult to decrease the achievement gaps with inequities of available resources.

Chapter 11

WHEN LATE SPRING arrived, Ms. Barbara Williams, my assistant principal, who would later take over as principal, called me in with a new challenge. "The district leaders planned to announce a summer creative arts program, a teenage performing arts workshop (TAPAW). Your license is in speech and theater, correct?"

I nodded even though the certification had been useless at 35. She cornered me with an offer sensing I could not refuse. "I want our kids off the streets. So how about something new and fresh not some borrowed script used every year by some school. How about you create an original play? Use our kids and keep them busy for the summer. I've got resources to make it happen, so I'll fund you and I'll give you a staff."

She proposed that I write, direct, and present a play that could showcase any kid: the gifted and talented neighborhood students, not necessarily the kids from my previous classes but rather, any students from the school, as well as students from neighboring districts willing to attend a six-week summer program. Often, we witnessed youngsters demonstrate artistic talent in dance or song or acting regardless of academic standing. Our school also labeled some students "SP", the intellectually gifted groups who I never taught but knew from homeroom class.

"Can I think about it?"

Dismayed by my hesitation, she pushed a bit, and her actions reminded me of Principal Dembo who assumed I would and could teach for his school. "You wanted theater or speech, so here's a challenge *and* the salary is quite good. We have a grant. You won't be alone, I 've got a great staffing idea for this."

I felt somewhat pushed to accept the position and could always use the summer financial bonus. This challenge would test my creativity an, my ability to work with a more diverse student population. Maybe I could earn working with a class with higher-level kids.

"I'm in."

I accepted the position writer/director and would work alongside a team including: set designer, choreographer, music director. All three teaching colleagues, except for a fourth hired professional stage manager, could fit the pieces neatly together. So, while completing a successful school year, I embarked on my new project. I brainstormed, tossed around numerous ideas, and eventually wrote a script for "Hurdlin'", a musical journey covering 1920s through 1970s that highlighted the Roaring Twenties, the Great Depression, World War II, the good time 50s, the turbulent 60s and 70s, including the Civil Rights Movement and Vietnam. Written in rhyme, like today's rap, the melodic lines could be memorized easily by struggling readers who loved music and might want to test their dramatic abilities. The subject matter taught history lessons in a unique style that celebrated the arts.

One mid-June morning, I submitted my draft to Ms. Williams for approval before perfecting the script.

"Love it! We'll get the ball rolling and start with morning announcements and spark some interest." She grinned.

She passed it back, setting me free to begin my newest adventure. I set out to encourage a variety of pupils who struggled with academic success but possessed interest, talent, and creativity. The original script moved decade by decade and my colleagues created accompanying music, dance routines and scenery to emphasize the messages. It was one of the first of its kind in New York City. By the week's end, we slapped posters in local store windows and stapled them on telephone poles attempting to recruit any interested players. We knew during summers in the city, kids had too much idle time, so the program offered a healthy option. Enough kids memorized song lyrics, could rhyme, or dance and proudly take center stage, as well as avoid the lure of street life.

That first week of the program, right after July 4th weekend, we held auditions: two strong narrators, a cast of actors with major or minor speaking roles, singers for both soloists and chorus, dancers and musicians and volunteer artists for set design. The try-outs began and the lines of students were encouraging. Talent flowed through the neighborhood. Over seventy volunteers wanted to participate so casting was not an issue. The pool of candidates ranged from sixth graders, age eleven to about freshmen/sophomores ages fifteen to sixteen. My team collectively separated the groups, debated, and made final cuts from the wealth of varying abilities we saw.

We posted the list complete with roles and understudies. We doled out parts and watched the creativity blossom. We chose from a plethora of talent and discovered actors, singers, dancers, musicians, artists. Young musicians worked under our band/musical director, Mr. Wedlaw, a hip guy whose musical accompaniment brought my story to life. He recruited strong brass players, a prolific drummer and included a few ringers who had graduated but kept in contact with the talented director. I still recall how the music roared through the practice rooms. A local group of teen artists assisted set designer Mr. Castagna by sketching unique scenes rather than spend their summer mornings practicing graffiti. The dancers learned from Ms. Broussard, a talented choreographer whose artistic pieces represented each era and challenged the students as they practiced new steps. Whether the roots were African, Southern melodies or reflections of Harlem and the North, they danced the messages with pride and skill. I directed, worked lines and positioning. And a professional stage manager, Fred Seagraves, manipulated lighting and sound to assure the best product. The grant provided ample funding for professional costumes, and we rented appropriate outfits that matched each decade's ideas. We may all have acknowledged that keeping kids off the streets equaled less time for finding trouble and kept a neighborhood quieter during steamy conditions. But we witnessed something special as kids found purpose and gave 110% day after day as their confidence grew.

During auditions, knowing Forrest was so smart, I hoped he would appear, but he was nowhere to be found when the summer program commenced. I feared that theater arts didn't mesh with the Hellcat mentality anyway, but I dared to hope. Unfortunately, he was missing the entire summer, maybe on vacation and though I worried, I was preoccupied with work duties, swarmed by different students, enthusiastic performers.

Rehearsals continued five days a week, nine until noon, when heat forced us to stop. Occasionally, we ran longer and divided mandatory times depending upon the scheduled scene work, but no one complained. We offered a simple snack of fruit and chips and a cool water fountain to help survive the stuffy, non-air-conditioned building including an auditorium with poor ventilation and some music rooms in the basement for morning sessions. They were sometimes overheated but always hungry learners who mastered everything we fed them. When administrators observed what we did, they offered a compromise.

"We are relocating the final production to take place at Wingate." All cheered with the prospect of performing in a cooled local high school auditorium after suffering through six weeks.

A colleague from the science department brought her son to audition. He joined us that summer and became the most unforgettable artist I encountered. During rehearsals, I noticed that little Larry was a natural who magnetically drew onlookers to his spot on the stage whenever he uttered a line. His ability to deliver his lines with eloquence demonstrated a stage presence not comparable to his peers. Although I did not assign him head narrator role because he was only eleven, he stole every scene and highlighted the show. I regretted my casting error from day one.

After summer ended, Larry, our young prodigy worked with The Negro Ensemble Co., soon became a professional and secured a leading role in the film, "Cornbread, Earl and Me". Driven by a stage mom, he rode the fast track to greatness. About three years later, Frances Ford Coppola must have agreed with my talent assessment. He made a similar discovery and casted the tall fourteen-year-old Larry in "Apocalypse Now" in which he played an eighteen-year-old soldier with a memorable scene listening to the Rolling Stones while traveling down the Mekong Delta during the Vietnam War. Instantly, he became a Hollywood pick for his unforgettable performance. No longer called Larry, he was billed under his birth name, Laurence Fishburne. Decades later, recognized as a consummate actor, he earned an Oscar nomination for his brilliance as "Othello". For a few years, I chose to use clips from his film while teaching the Shakespearean play to my sophomores. I boasted about being one of his first directors and posted his picture on my bulletin board, alongside my favorite family photos. Finally, thirty-six years after our summer work, I reunited with Mr. Laurence Fishbourne, once my little Larry, after watching his brilliant one-man Broadway performance, "Thurgood". Although I am rarely at a loss for words, I stood dumbstruck and let my husband Ronnie become my voice when Mr. Fishbourne graciously invited me to his dressing room after a theater usher passed him my personal note complete with his "Hurdling" head shot from 1971. I am not sure he remembered who I was, but he agreed to pose for a photo with me and teary-eyed, I completed my awesome journey.

"Hurdlin'" was a huge success. Even my mother and father agreed to leave their haven to witness our efforts. They traveled the outdated, winding Interboro Parkway to an unfamiliar Brooklyn neighborhood to sit in the standing room-only Wingate High School auditorium. And a few of my Brooklyn-based relatives added to the overflowing attendance. We performed to a packed house of relatives, friends, and folks from the neighborhood out for a free night of entertainment. Thoroughly awed and delighted for two hours, onlookers witnessed a small piece of what made my profession so rewarding. My elated students beamed and bowed in response to the continuous standing ovations and roaring applause. We did a good job that summer and even made the local news! Never underestimate!

Even today, I can recite the opening intro:

I'm gonna take you through the past
Cuz the world is changing mighty fast
Watch the clothes, hairdos, and the music too,
Change from corny and old to "bad" and new.
Look at the faces, Check out the places.
See which time was really the best, the times you think above the rest.
I'll take you from the 20s right up to today,
So, sit back, relax, and hear what I say!

Chapter 12

UNFORTUNATELY, WHEN I needed a breather, I realized that the six-week summer assignment eliminated any time to revitalize and about two weeks after my successful theater production, I returned to JHS 35 for the start of a new school year. That was the one and only time I accepted summer employment after the realization that the two-month hiatus helped reenergize me and fine-tune my batteries for September's opening dates.

Forrest returned, but never shared his summer experiences with me. Although he often held his head down and avoiding looking at people, he appeared happy to reconnect with me. He began each day by checking in early before the school day began, stopping by between classes, and ending eighth period in my room to discuss the day's events. He graduated to morning and afternoon visits and only one period of reading instruction in room 216. After the successful prior year with me, administrators grafted him into a more typical schedule expecting other teachers might now have better luck with him since his in-school behavior significantly improved. In the outside world, I feared that adults in his life ignored his needs, but he felt wanted in my room. He never desired to go home, never talked about family, just followed my lead like a puppy.

By this time in my career, I realized my gift as a nurturer. I was never the sharpest or smartest faculty member, but I thought no one cared for students more than me. I tried to touch all who sat in my classrooms. With Forrest, I knew how to build his confidence, direct his energies and I refused to give up. It was evident that where everyone else initially saw desperation, I saw promise. Although he didn't speak much, his body language, as well as his written language, said it all. His tough exterior still showed others an arrogance and defiance, but still a child, he yearned for attention and acknowledgement.

As my personal project, I worked diligently to soften Forrest's hardened heart without making him feel weak. He needed his posturing for survival and the reality was that when 3:00 p.m. arrived, he returned to the streets and his unsavory cohorts who rarely considered the consequences of their actions and thought themselves invincible. Many bounced in and out of juvie and appeared like wanderers always searching. Yet, Forrest was a born leader and I hoped eventually he could redirect his negative behavior and either influence others to retreat from dangerous choices or leave them behind. At the time, he never shared his criminal activities with me or complained about the lack of family involvement in his development. I never pried, but I suspected.

Incidents in the classroom continued to challenge my knowledge and knowhow. I recall a day in one class where a student's offensive body odor interfered with the behavior and productivity of her classmates who refused to work with her on assignments.

"She stinks, and I'm not sitting near her!"

"Enough! Cut the nonsense!"

They quieted but not for long and continuously embarrassed the girl. To set the example, I attempted to model behavior and stop their insults, but even I could not cope with this situation as I was forced to breathe through my mouth until the period ended. I guessed that the lack of bathing and wearing of unwashed clothing were the culprits and by reporting this to the nurse, I could manage the problem. I was wrong.

According to Forrest, my assumption was incorrect.

"The young lady can't get hair products. She's using old bacon grease that stinks."

He informed me that she created a pomade from leftover morning bacon grease that mixed with a day of personal sweat, resulting in a rancid odor. Although she washed her hair about once a week or so, the mixture's odor permeated the room and worsened from Monday to Friday.

"You wanna help her? Get her some products. I'll show you what you need."

I agreed and after school we, an unlikely pair to observers, shopped at a local drug store where Forrest offered a few suggestions. Shampoos, conditioners, and detanglers by Afro-Sheen, a brand designed to treat all types of ethnic hair, filled my cart. Then we moved down another aisle and he pointed to the lotions and moisturizers suitable for drier skin.

"Coco butter, or shea butter," he suggested.

I put one of each into the cart. As a clerk rang up the items, Forrest watched me closely, wondering if I would pick up the bill once it was totaled.

"I got this," I nodded, and he half-grinned in approval.

After I privately presented the recipient with a shopping bag filled with purchased products suitable for both her hair and body cleaning, *poof!* The sickening smells disappeared from her hair and body almost immediately. A bit embarrassed, she acknowledged my involvement and before long, everything about her changed. As her offensive odor disappeared, her confidence emerged. Once again, Forrest's smarts taught me a great lesson.

Poverty deterred many of my students from replacing worn clothing or alternating outfits. Yet, many moms washed shirts and underwear by hand religiously so that their offspring appeared neater than some of their disheveled peers. Laundromats, although costly, flourished since most homes were devoid of washers and dryers.

Forrest was rarely clean since daily showers or baths were not part of his ritual at his sister's or when sleeping in hallways or on trains. Still, he never arrived in tattered clothes. I learned years later about his housing dilemma and discovered that shoplifting from the local department store, Abraham & Strauss (A & S), was a regular habit that provided his wardrobe essentials. Pride did not allow him to confess his issues at the time even though he knew I often bought apparel for needy students. Never a taker, handouts were taboo, according to his standards.

Chapter 13

BY MY SECOND or third year of back and forth on the Interboro, the Sunbeam Alpine went to car heaven after many repairs and breakdowns were killing my pocketbook. It was replaced with a yellow VW bug that resembled a wasp with its black trim and interior. Spanking new, it was mine for about one month when I discovered it missing one morning from a parking space diagonally across the street from my Carlyle Towers luxury apartment. Funny, the robbery occurred in my "safe Flushing neighborhood", not in the unsavory neighborhood where I spent five or six days every week. Insurance reimbursed me and the yellow was replaced with a red Super Beetle. I do remember that no one in Bed Stuyvesant vandalized the Beetle. Many of my colleagues' cars discovered their rides marred on a daily basis. It all depended upon which tough guy was mad at which teacher. Fortunately, Forrest's rules of keeping me safe persisted; I was untouchable.

Many Saturday excursions exposed my non-athletic self to sports when I accompanied Forrest as he explored worlds outside of his neighborhood. A few times we bowled although he never knew that it remains one of my least favorite forms of entertainment. No matter how I held that heavy ball, where I stood left or right side of the lane or how I aimed, I rolled the ball at a snail's pace, and it inevitably landed in the gutter.

"Whew Miss, you're terrible."

After he unsuccessfully attempted to straighten my right wrist throughout the ten frames, I earned low scores that ranged from 9 to 59. Forrest, on the other hand, with youth and agility on his side, found this a fun activity and fared well. So, we bowled, and we laughed at my incompetence and his sharp aim. Forty years later, I once again participate in a sport I dislike on rare occasions with my grandkids.

Basketball was not new to Forrest. It was a free game to inner city youth, so he was a baller. There were no fees to play and if one kid in the neighborhood shared the ball, games went on until dark. Often, the hoops were just rims with torn or no nets and the courts were littered with garbage—drug paraphernalia, alcohol bottles or litter soda cans left by transients who disregarded safety, health, and environmental concerns. But anyone could play on any available court. Forrest joined games on our better-kept Flushing courts where he said little and sweat plenty. Not a competitor, I sat nearby, dividing my time between reading, and watching, but I never offered pointers or volunteered input, simply waited for the games to end when I provided a towel, and he wiped his perspiration and we moved on.

As usual, afterwards, we snacked or shared a bite at a local spot. On a couple of occasions, Forrest and I trekked back to the apartment, where he washed up and cooled down before rerouting back to his neighborhood. His disposition changed when we prepared to journey back. Reality interrupted the day's fun, which he understood had to end when we ventured back to Brooklyn, letting the radio break the uncomfortable silence.

Twice, the routine changed. With permission from his sister who didn't ever seem too concerned about his whereabouts, Forrest spent the night on my living room couch and returned to Brooklyn early the following morning. With a soft pillow under his head, blanketed with a cushy comforter, he required little to make him happy other than a bit of my attention. During that era, teachers nurtured differently. It was not shocking to learn about a sleepover. He was surprised by my inability to cook, something my mother never taught me because in her obsessive-compulsive state about cleanliness, she refused to allow me to experiment and possibly dirty her immaculate stove. I remember once making a chart with my sister of all the food storage cabinets as well as the order of pots and pans stored in the lower stove drawer so that when she was out and I was "experimenting", I could return everything to its proper place. After two attempts to get over on her, I gave up culinary arts: once, I ate an entire tray of chocolate cupcakes to erase evidence and was quickly nauseated. A second time, Max and I baked brownies, ate our full, opened windows to eliminate any chocolate aroma and buried the extras in the backyard. After preparing pasta for a snack, Mom found one strand of hardened spaghetti wedged under a burner despite my cleaning attempt—as a result, my cooking career ended.

Forrest knew about takeout and fast food and constantly shook his head at the simple kitchen and housecleaning etiquette that I never mastered. He could clean a table or sink better than me and demonstrated this often, never sitting idle to be catered to and always assisting in any preparation or cleanup. I recall one instance when he helped me create my family meal before my parents' arrival. I decided to prepare brisket of beef, just like Mama. It would be the perfect fit, so I used a family recipe and Forrest was my sous chef. After watching me cut carrots in my inept way, fearing for my safety, he removed the knife from my hands and proceeded to give me lessons in dicing vegetables, as well as directions in the art of knife safety.

"NEVER CUT TOWARDS YOUR HAND WITH A KNIFE IN THE AIR! You're gonna cut yourself! And you're gonna choke your folks if you keep the carrots that big!"

Shaking his head, he added, "Don't you know how to season?"

Then, he seasoned the meat, asking me why I didn't understand what a pinch of salt, pepper or garlic meant as he surmised that the meal would be disastrous without his expertise. I still laugh at his imitation of how I clobbered carrots and how he cringed thinking I would lose my fingertips and leave them as a garnish around the meat.

With little words, his expressions softened, and his fondness shone through. Whether it was the first box of chocolates or the tiger's eye ring or the broken ceramic Christmas gift, or the cooking lessons, they all were love offerings. Thirty-five years later, only the ring remains and when I tell students about Forrest, I wear it to school as concrete proof of my stories. Sadly, I have no photographic memories from those days since he rejected picture taking because of his twisted eye, but in my mind, I clearly see the special young man who I lost like the prodigal son only to be found at a later time.

Decades later, I shared the long story about my life with Forrest with Hala Hourani, a dear friend who responded: "Our best teachers are our students, and he had, by all of your accounts, valuable lessons to teach, one of the most significant being that theory and ideology are the poorest voices for the harsh realities experienced by many of the faces we encounter on our journey as educators."

Witnessing so many inequities during those Brooklyn years, I hoped for a world free from institutional racism and poverty. I sought change as I listened to student voices and heard of their plights through their writings. I wanted and attempted to become an advocate for not only children of color, but also, for the any of the ignored, the disenfranchised and the undocumented students that would cross my path.

Chapter 14

IN THE SPRING of 1975, a strikingly handsome, athletic-looking man arrived at JHS 35 to substitute. His unique stature took my breath away. To me, he was Michelangelo's David, a chiseled piece of perfection: soft brown curly hair, European styled close-cut full beard, skin a shade resembling coffee with cream, deep brown, soulful eyes, a crooked smile, and a perfectly crafted physique. He was impeccably groomed, looked like a magazine cover. Tall, over 6 feet, his presence seemed to erase everything around him. For me, it was like a movie scene where the center focus blurs the rest of the frame. One glance in the office, one quick acknowledgement of "Hello", and my stomach dropped. I was smitten.

While punching my attendance timecard following the brief encounter with Mr. Right, curiosity got the best of me. Without advertising my interest, I perused the office paperwork, the substitute teacher list, which revealed a name: Ronnie Nunn. And an asterisk notation: STRONG—CALL DAILY. Rumors spread, including his ability to discipline his classes, manage and relate to students seemingly without effort.

While over-hearing the school gossips in the female breakroom, one colleague who also appreciated his good looks, announced, "Have you seen the new sub, Ronnie Nunn? That man could cause infidelity!"

After unison laughter, another responded, "He's a hottie." The group unanimously agreed. "I heard his mother is Italian and father is African American. Whatever he is, it works!" chimed in another.

We all agreed that he could pass for Native American, Latino, Greek, Middle Eastern, Israeli, which would have pleased my mother. I knew that I was smitten and eager to move on in my life either with a new partner or alone. Not the least bit apprehensive, aware that it was time for change, I dared to change everything! Like the song, "Just one look, that's all it took."

During his first week of work, his scheduler assigned second floor hall duty, walking back and forth on monotonous patrol at the same time one of my class periods in room 216. Truly, I may sound like a stalker, but I had no intention of pursuing if he was not interested or turned out to be a player who wanted conquests rather than relationships. Conveniently, I positioned myself in the opened doorway after assigning silent reading passages to my students who sat confused over a sudden, new format. The school custom usually was to close the steel windowless door, but I convinced them that in this late April morning, we needed ventilation. I lied. As he passed through the swinging double doors fifteen feet before my room, our eyes linked and a conversation ensued.

"Looks like you've got that class in order," he complimented after glancing into the room and witnessing the group's conduct. "You must be some teacher or maybe, being attractive gives you an edge."

According to him, I probably mesmerized the young boys who dared not misbehave in my room. Laughing, I acknowledged his attention and for a few minutes, was frozen in time. As we mildly flirted, my insides were fluttering. I felt like a teenager, not a twenty-seven-year-old who had baggage and a long-time partner since college. Unsettled and unhappy with my present situation, I knew that life changes were imminent. I had grown apart from my partner and knew I could no longer live a lie.

Boldly, we agreed to meet during the following period lunch to continue to talk.

Appearing poised, I turned my attention to the students and ignored snide remarks while others smirked at the "secret" flirtation they witnessed. "Hey, one day I might marry that fine hall patrol teacher!" I kidded.

They roared and hooted as we shared a good laugh and returned to the day's assignment. Thirty minutes later, I attempted to save him a seat in the small lunchroom, but we were without privacy, as the regulars at the long cafeteria table surrounded me. He selected another table, sat alone assuming I was busy chatting. But somehow, I impulsively managed to pass him a note containing my personal contact information. It was guised in approach about a disorderly student.

"Here's the telephone contact numbers for that boy's parents. I would call sooner than later and get him in order."

I pushed the note into his hand and though he was clueless about my messaging, he played along. "Got it," he nodded as if he understood my intentions.

I suspected that my personal life was about to change, and after some harmless past flirtations with others, I was finally ready to separate myself from my present relationship even though I was terrified being the aggressor for the first time. Leaving my old life and starting fresh, I comprehended that this situation would impact my life forever. The folded note informed him of my early school arrivals, suggesting we meet for coffee and a chat. Unfortunately, I was unaware at the time, Mr. Nunn's inner clock resulted in perpetual lateness and any morning rendezvous was close to impossible. So, much to my dismay, he was a no-show that week. Yet, within days, when I appeared less interested and dismissive, the pursued became a pursuer and he arrived for the morning chat a bit after 7:00 a.m. red-eyed and half asleep to meet clandestinely before classes commenced.

His intentions probably never included long-term commitments, but I thought differently. I later discovered that his initial goal was to meet many women, enjoy the party scene, and keep his status as uninvolved as possible. After all, a plethora of attractive, single ladies occupied JHS 35, many of whom desired his attention. He also learned of my attachment and looking back, he probably thought he'd have a brief dalliance or conquest and then explore other opportunities. We kept our morning rendezvous secret, so my competitors believed he was free to reel in, an available catch. He was as cool as they come and gregarious enough to keep many of them dangling until the reality of my next move hit him.

Three days after the first morning encounter, I stunned him when I passed him a note as he coincidentally taught in an adjacent room. "I packed up my former life and left the relationship this morning." I stuffed my essentials into one lone suitcase and left my life in Flushing, never to look back.

"You're kidding, right?" he questioned after the bell ended class and he stood, blocking my door. "Where are you going? Do you need help?"

I nodded and said little at the time. I knew he was in shock, but he drove me home to pick up some extra things before dropping me off at my sister's apartment.

Initially my sister, Max, came to the rescue offering me a pull-out couch and a haven until I could straighten out my life and become less unsettled. In her small Queens apartment, she protected me by intercepting various telephone calls from family members eager for explanations about my erratic behavior. Informing them that I was safe, but not ready to entertain conversations, she eased tension and offered silent support. Flooded with calls from my blood relatives, as well as my ex's relatives, Max shielded me and took the heat. I don't think to this day she realizes how grateful I felt. She never badgered me with inquiry, but rather, stood beside me during a scary time. I left a secure life for an uncertain future, no promised happiness, but I knew I could no longer be content living unfulfilled.

So, I closed one door, wiped my feet, and began a new terrifying chapter without guarantees. I took the plunge hoping to swim rather than sink, hoping that my instincts were correct, and that chemistry could overpower my spontaneous actions. For about six weeks, I depended upon Max and took advantage of my sister's generosity and her couch until I house-sat for a while and later could sublet an apartment and begin again.

I still traveled to work daily, even had Ronnie pick me up and drive me in a few times to avoid mass transit. His time management skills, though, caused a few late arrivals much out of the ordinary for punctual me and some faculty members suspected that we were involved.

"Mr. Nunn, I know you're seeing Andee because that young woman hasn't been late once in five years. Until now. You've got to get her here on time."

The daily scheduler Mr. Smith, aka Smitty, needled Ronnie with the warning. Because our relationship was still a clandestine one, he tried his best to get me to work on time from that day forward. We were getting to know one another while I completed two months of the school year at JHS 35.

My priorities shifted. I focused more on changing my personal life, but I never neglected my students while in the building. Forrest, now older, aware his years at JHS 35 were ending soon, took advantage of the flexible attendance policy during the last months, arrived late and even missed a few of the ten days permitted each year before loss of academic credit. When Forrest learned about Ronnie, he was less than thrilled. He was maturing and didn't like sharing me with a new stranger. Ronnie, after a brief introduction, watched from afar and hinted that Forrest was becoming a man, no longer the little boy I once nurtured. He sensed that the teen acted too possessively, and I should be aware of possible consequences. After all, he was considerably older than his classmates and donned a moustache, validating his entrance into manhood. His comment was a bit unsettling. The school year was closing, so I dismissed the warning.

At the time, Ronnie, just tempted by some short-term entertainment, thought I was bonkers, but he was intrigued. Later, he shared that he was frightened with uncertainty being interested in an attached woman who left a man for him! I was also two years older than him and Jewish. This was unprecedented. We spent endless hours together and on top of the physical attraction, we liked each other's company. We laughed often, shared yummy food at 110 Mott Street, a local Chinatown spot, confessed our histories and couldn't get enough of each other. Although I dove into the relationship, Ronnie was reluctant and had his own baggage, a long-time girlfriend from the neighborhood and a college lover, as well. I hadn't been privy to this before, but I assumed that two love interests meant neither met all his needs, so I pursued the relationship. He played "love ping-pong" for years, but now, ending that game, he spent most of his time with me. The whirlwind continued. We remained a couple for the remainder of the school year.

For the final months of the school year, students and Forrest filled my weekdays, but situations were on the verge of altering. My homelife took my focus away from Brooklyn on the weekends as I built my life with Ronnie, but in school, I noticed erratic changes in Forrest. I remember his terrier, Whiskey, who he fed a combination of dog food and hot sauce before leaving the house.

"I gotta keep him mean!" he reasoned. "Then assholes stay away."

I tried to stop him, to no avail. After time, hints about his home life surfaced and needed addressing. I learned that Forrest's mother, accompanied by the younger siblings, permanently relocated leaving him with an older sister, but he fended for himself. Mom's intention was for him eventually to follow her South, but he remained in Brooklyn. I am unsure of why his living situation with his older sister failed. I think a boyfriend caused friction. I just knew he had nowhere to go, and I surmised that he would end up in the street. I uncovered the truth, and the uncomfortable news led me to search for a solution that would remedy his unsettling reality. When I discovered that Forrest spent much of his time alone, I made it my business to either provide him with company or deliver him to friends or relatives. He lived a slippery slope, and I did not learn until 2009 that many nights he rode trains, slept in hallways and on park benches during that tumultuous time.

So many years we shared part of our lives together and he never complained. Although he locked away secrets too difficult to reveal, it was evident that his living conditions deteriorated. He appeared unkempt and hungry, and his face hinted signs of sleeplessness. I kept questioning but got few responses. I prodded and I uncovered a possible solution. He had another relative, an aunt located on Long Island, so

I insisted he reach out to her. When his mother's sister learned of her nephew's plight, she agreed to relocate him to her Freeport home.

"It's a good option," I tried to offer advice.

"I gotta leave my boys? Go to some country bumpkin spot? And how the hell am I supposed to do that?"

"I'll take you. I know Long Island, remember? It's about a half hour from where I grew up. It's nice out there and you'll have family. You can go to school with your cousins, make new friends and live better."

I tried to sound reassuring and although he was skeptical, he conceded because the alternatives options were limited to subway or hallway sleeping, resulting in getting picked up by police and probably ending in juvie again. I think the loneliness became overwhelming, too. Forrest gathered his belongings all fitting into two brown paper grocery bags and we traveled in sporadic silence to the first home where he might feel safe, connected, and embraced by extended family.

During the ride, I tried to explain in an upbeat manner how both of us were embarking on new lives. "This is a new beginning for both of us! You can go to Freeport High, get a diploma, and then decide to go to a college, or in the Army or get a good job. You will have choices with a degree. My life is changing too. You know I moved and am starting over."

He did not respond, not a nod or a blink. Reality was that I was physically driving him to suburban Long Island, a far cry from the Bedford Stuyvesant streets that he knew. He would no longer grace my presence at JHS 35, no longer be physically near me. Armed with all he taught me, I knew I could master the classroom alone. It took over five years, but I had skills.

My recollection is foggy, but later I learned that his was crystal clear. I recall a tearful goodbye. I reiterated how this was a turning point.

"This is your ticket for a new beginning and place to better your life." I remained upbeat and reassuring as my eyes welled up and I hugged him. His body was stiff, ungiving and defiant and he said nothing. I got in my car, rolled down the window and spoke. "Give it a chance, Forrest. You got this! You have my number and need to stay in touch, so I know you're well. Promise to check in and call, okay?"

He nodded without looking directly at me. He pivoted and sauntered towards the house never looking back. It was unsettling for me, but sadly, I drove away.

Chapter 15

DURING THE SUMMER my relationship with Ronnie became all-inclusive and by September, I moved into a Park Slope apartment. Accepting an unspoken invitation, Ronnie moved into an apartment with me, and we began our life together.

One evening in late 1976 during one of my many train excursions leaving Chinatown and returning to my Park Slope rental, Ronnie, now my fiancé, and I met old acquaintances. Our intention was to enjoy a late turn-around dinner trip from Brooklyn to New York City where restaurants still served at 11:00 p.m. Then we would board the F train a little after midnight and return home. This was nothing new to us since the thirty-minute train ride offered convenience over searching for parking on crowded, narrow streets of lower Manhattan. Despite the hour, we never anticipated problems, knowing that occasional subway incidents occurred at later hours typically not on the F train but more commonly on the A train or other trains that traveled through tougher neighborhoods. Naturally, I understood "subway etiquette rituals" from Forrest.

"Check out the car, sit where there are no blind spots, scan the crowd, but never stare at anyone so you ain't a victim. You never know which guy's face is on a wanted poster in the post office." His rules.

So, I felt safe and in good company sitting beside my big protector who also knew subways. Years before college, Ronnie's daily rides from his home to Brooklyn Technical High School, as well as journeying to all parts of the city for basketball games, made him a mass transit pro. Yet about ten minutes into our return trip, I sensed a change. Ronnie's body language instinctively hinted discomfort when the doors opened and a disorderly herd of foul- mouthed, loud male teens pushed into the car creating immediate havoc. Their body language suggested teens on a rampage, possibly stealing, mugging, and intimidating others in a mob-style manner. Later, the term, "wilding", was coined to describe this behavior more accurately.

Ronnie went into planning and calculating mode. His mind spun. How do we escape harm? Which one of these thugs would he grab, threaten, and hurt, if necessary, to protect not only himself, but also, his vulnerable partner, me? Outnumbered and fearing for our safety, he mumbled, "Listen, I know this train. I know the stops. If we need to move, I got you. And if I have to go for one of them, I will."

I sensed unsettling drama to say the least. He scared me. At this late hour, only a handful of commuters sat in the car. I witnessed them immediately shrink in their seats, heads down, hoping to not become targets before they could flee the pending doom. With menacing laughter, the gang flashed money, swung around the poles, boldly jutted chest-first towards an elderly couple and feigned attack on passengers. Puffed up, they staggered down the aisles, swearing, staring, daring, darting, and threatening. Nearing like prowlers in search of prey, they inched closer. I could almost hear hearts racing with anxiety. Ronnie nudged.

"Sit tight," he quietly warned, insisting I ignore the predators but wait for his cue to bolt if doors opened. He knew the distances between all stops, as well as how long doors typically stayed open for travelers to enter or exit cars. His hand grabbed my wrist ready to pull.

Anxiously, awaiting direction, I heard one of the voices, a familiar one. I knew not to stare but I scanned the crowd and spotted Speedy, one of Forrest's cohorts, another former Hellcat. Speedy was his gang name and his history included violence. While the train travelers cringed, Speedy sauntered down the aisle towards my direction with the swarm following close behind him. Ronnie's hand tightened in a signal to prepare for a problem, to follow his guiding hand, but the unexpected occurred. In a tone filled with kind authority, my voice instantaneously emerged. "Speedy, is that you?"

Hearing his name, he appeared startled and stopped dead in his tracks.

"Just what are you supposed to be doing?"

I was now boldly standing, confronting him.

Our eyes locked when I called him out. I hoped and prayed that my act would work in this unfamiliar territory. This was not the classroom. Was the power still present? Cold eyes warmed, actually sparkled, and his sly smile cracked as a different personality emerged. The leader removed his hat just like Forrest did on day one. He extended his hand and adjusted his demeanor. "Miss Phillips! Is that you? Wow, yo boys, this is Forrest's special lady!"

The handshake changed to a hug. His eyes darted.

"Is this Mr. Phillips?"

Poof! The tense atmosphere vanished, and dialogue began as I introduced the head honcho to Ronnie, my fiancé and then chastised him for his inappropriate behavior and intentions.

"Sorry Ms. Phillips, my bad. We don't mean nothing."

He apologized, nodded to "his boys" who obeyed his directions and suddenly, the seas calmed! Everyone in the car, old and young, breathed a bit easier as the chaos ceased.

Speedy chuckled. "Have you seen Satan…I mean Forest?"

"Not lately. You?" I responded with sadness.

"Dude's gone missing. Even Selina has no clue about her baby bro. We heard he was going into the service."

After brief exchanges, with salutations completed, he led his crew off two stops later probably to intimidate different targets. A stunned, harried group, including Ronnie, stared at me in amazement because it appeared to them that this little lady in miracle mode saved the day, but I knew better. Forrest's reputation protected me throughout Brooklyn wherever I traveled. His presence was not needed for him to do so.

Chapter 16

I MARRIED IN 1977 in Brooklyn Borough Hall on Friday, November 4th at 3:50 p.m. The time is significant because understanding that Ronnie always ran late, I told him that halls both in Manhattan and Brooklyn closed at 4:00 so he could manage his time. At 1:45 p.m., my maid of honor, Maxine, and Ronnie's closest friend and college roommate, our best man, Lennox, waited anxiously with the prospective bride for the prospective groom to appear. In truth, Lennox worried that Ronnie might be a no-show, but around 2:15, he arrived.

"Had to have the Buick cleaned for the special occasion. Took longer than expected, but we're good to go. Going to just change. Everyone is ready to move!"

No one answered him.

As usual, we raced to Chambers Street in Manhattan, the original destination where Ronnie hoped to repeat a ceremony performed there sanctioning his parents' interracial union in 1942. It would be a nostalgic moment. But with over one hundred couples online ahead of us, his wish could not be granted. There were so many folks waiting that Ronnie actually pointed to an elementary school buddy who he briefly greeted. All felt hopeless until a guard who monitored the traffic in the hallway suggested we reroute to Brooklyn because its courthouse never seemed to be as busy.

"You'll be in and out in no time."

Frankly, time was running out. My blood boiled as we sped in silence to reach our new destination and complete this union. After all, my parents were throwing a wedding celebration Saturday, the following day in Asbury Park, New Jersey and I refused Ronnie's other option to wait until Monday to exchange vows.

Thankfully, the guard was correct. We arrived within fifteen minutes with only one couple waiting before our turn. There were no romantic feelings reading the posted signs: NO THROWING RICE! HAVE PAPERWORK READY.

Finally, before a justice of the peace who directed his words calling me Ronnie and Ronnie, Andee until we corrected him. At last, we exchanged our vows at 3:50.

"See that, we had TEN minutes to spare!" my new husband boasted.

"Wrong! The place closes at 5:00 but knowing you and your timetable, I told you 4:00!"

That shocked him as he complained, "So, I got married under false pretenses."

Years later, he still barks that I lied on our wedding day.

After about a year as newlyweds, I sparked on a serious conversation. "I'm thirty-one. We should think about starting a family."

My "younger husband" who thought I robbed the cradle, conceded. He figured fatherhood was his next step, so I became pregnant and with protruding belly, I continued teaching until the semester ended June 1979, with two months to go until my firstborn.

Before moving on, I was determined to have a memorable field trip under my bulging belt. Forrest, living in Freeport, Long Island was not beside me, but I knew by now from numerous times together that I could handle my final hurrah. Pregnant, I announced my excitement to the world by wearing a silly T-shirt, "Baby" with an illustrated downward arrow. I boarded the subway heading to Coney Island's aquarium and beach. Like usual, I carried bagged lunches but also told students to save some change and experience the novelty of mouth-watering Nathan's boardwalk eatery. It offered hot dogs covered in spicy brown mustard, which snapped with each bite, incomparable crinkle-cut thick

French fries served in paper cones and unique square potato knishes, before the business became a New York staple and opened concessions in local malls and offered options in the frozen section of grocery chains.

This trip began during rush hour. First on an A train, followed by a change of train to the D into a crowded, standing room-only car that did not offer me and my huge seven-month pregnant belly a seat.

A student barked loudly, "I know one of you guys here are gonna give my teacher a seat!"

"Right?" his buddies yelled in unison.

Peering at people like Forrest used to do, the audience of riders were rocked by his cold stare and obeyed the command. At least five men in suits who previously ignored my condition, rose, scampered towards the next car, and fled from the seemingly tough Black kids on board! They roared, slapping each other at the quick response. I shook my head, sat with eyebrows raised but grinning ear to ear despite the unconventional way I gained my seat.

The plan had included visiting the aquarium, but our stay was short because my students were repelled by the fish odor that permeated the building.

"It stinks in here."

Their assessment: penguins are cute and walk funny, stingrays are sleek and freaky cool-looking, fish are fish large and small coming in lots of colors, but they had enough. Hearing their whining, we left prematurely and headed towards the second stop, the boardwalk. Noticing the Nathan's green sign, a few purchased icy lemonade, but many tried the fries and agreed with my previous recommendation.

"These fries are banging!"

"Let me get a few." Peers mooched when they could. But because of lack of funds, most waited for the school's packed lunches and scoffed food down in seconds. No wasting money on games though some were tempted to try and win a stuffed animal.

After walking for about fifteen minutes, they had enough, complaining about the heat. "Can we swim now?"

I nodded and we changed destination.

Coney Island's beach was heavenly. The sand was not beastly hot because summer heat had not penetrated yet, so they took off shoes and socks as they moved towards the water. Only a handful brought towels. The majority did not own bathing suits and they brought no change of clothes.

No one swam. Too many of my students feared the ocean because they did not know how to swim. They positioned themselves close to the water's edge, but more in the sand with cool water barely oozing through toes. Unfamiliar with riding waves like their teacher did before the enlarged belly interfered, they were content with the freedom, the sandcastles and getting splashed by rough breakers as they crashed. They screamed with elation as cool water flirted with their legs and set them running.

We heartily ate lunches and snacks, played, relaxed, and left mid-afternoon sated. They sat in damp, sand-filled clothing during the train ride home, and couldn't care less. An exhausted crew, half slept on the train while the remainder joked about desperately needing lotion to cover their skin affected by the region's salt water.

"Look at your ashy self!"

"Well, you got sand all in your braids, even in your ears!"

The innocent laughter filled the subway car. There were no confrontations or issues with outsiders as my contented crew traveled home to familiar territory. I sat smiling, witnessing the giggling innocence usually hidden by guarded exteriors. Although the day was a total success, I felt saddened knowing I'd be gone from their lives and uncertain about their futures.

Chapter 17

AS THE YEAR terminated, I left to exchange my teaching career for motherhood. Ten years in JHS 35 instructing over 1,250 students never prepared me for this next life phase. Frankly, I was overwhelmed.

On August 2, 1979, my daughter Ilana-Jes Phillips Nunn was born after eighteen hours of labor resulted in surgery. Ilana was a colic baby, a child that tested my sanity until her digestive system matured. After an unscheduled Caesarian delivery and a week's hospital stay, life in Brooklyn ended as mother and baby relocated to Port Chester the day after the hospital released us. Prior to leaving, Ronnie moved our packed belongings that I prepared weeks before giving birth. Now, he drove me and our precious cargo to our new two-bedroom spot in a renovated building in Port Chester, Westchester County.

Recovering from last-minute surgery, I needed to heal. Instead, I worked furiously unpacking ninety-one boxes to organize the new place with a newborn strapped to my chest. With her unsettled belly and a new soy formula, Ilana's daily routine included repeated bouts of projectile vomiting that literally left evidence all over the apartment and sleeplessness that forced car rides at all hours, day and night, since she found the movement slightly soothing. When out of ideas, I tried long walks on windy days both pushing and pulling the carriage traveling in one direction with air blowing in her face, which seemed to silence her. If for any part of the walk, wind blew behind her, the crying resumed.

I looked like a crazy lady pulling a child behind me turning my head back and forth to direct my path and watch Ilana.

Needless to say, year one was more than difficult. Could I survive the initial sleepless years and mold my daughter into a loveable child? Thankfully, by year two with a more settled tummy and healed ear canals, she slept six to eight hours, just about through the night. Shocked by the unbroken silence, it took a few more months for me to relax and sleep a few hours at a time without checking to see if she was breathing and alive.

Ilana morphed into a delightful, curly-topped, little angel at two. We moved again, renting a home from Ronnie's high school baseball catcher in a family-oriented neighborhood, but before I could get used to the glory and the quiet, Ilana's baby sister arrived to repeat the same hideous behavior and deprive me of the brief period of normalcy that flirted with me for a few months before her birth. I hoped for a better experience. It was a planned pregnancy because I believed in sibling support and was the product of such a relationship. A new doctor decided I could deliver this child without surgery but changed his mind after twenty-four hours of torture. Another C-section procedure, déjà vu.

Alexi-Vita Cammarata Nunn, my perfect baby, graced my life in 1982. Echoes of years before returned as another soy-fed child began her bout with irritable bowel and interrupted sleep in the household. Zombie Mom returned and lived within me for a little over a year. I knew the drill and coped until the storms ended. The girls both tested my sanity and filled my heart. The sisters grew close, became one another's best buddy playing endless hours occupying themselves, sharing childhoods and becoming major forces in their fields.

Although today, they are my greatest achievements, two accomplished, educated women, the endless hours of frustration suffered during their first years almost convinced me that I, the consummate teacher, was a failure as a mother. I look back, pat myself on the back and acknowledge that I survived the hurdles and did a pretty decent job.

Chapter 18

ALTHOUGH THE STORY is mainly about teaching and not family, my life involves a ten-year hiatus from the classroom, which warrants explanation. Ronnie's past successes in athletics, especially basketball, led to new endeavors. His hopes of playing basketball professionally finally ended after struggles with health took him out of the running. My girls became my projects while my husband juggled jobs to keep me a stay-at-home mom. Although sleep-deprived, every day, Ronnie taught special education in Pleasantville, which entitled us to medical benefits and a future pension. Two nights per week, he tended bar working into the wee hours of the early morning. Though I honestly detested the nightclub business, I knew that the pile of extra money grew and eventually became the nest-egg down payment for our first home. And he soon added a third job: assistant basketball coach at Pace University in Pleasantville, New York. Since basketball was in his blood, it was a perfect fit for him.

With Alexi's arrival in 1982 came job number four when Ronnie was approached by Cecil Watkins, his newest mentor and supporter. Cecil, who worked for the NBA, coaxed Ronnie into exploring the art of officiating. "If you've got the talent and the drive I think you have, I can make you a candidate for a position with the NBA. It's an opportunity to get on the court again and lead a good life. We need officials from minority groups, so if you work hard, learn the rules and referee as many games as you can, I think you'll be a viable candidate."

Initially, he rejected the offer, but as Cecil dangled the carrot assuring him that the league was looking for a more diverse staff, the proposition became more appealing. Determined, Ronnie spent weekend days on basketball courts both indoors and outdoors, all over New York and New Jersey honing his skills and earning pocket change. Robotically he changed clothes and traveled from job to job, but officiating became more of a real goal. Cecil observed and mentored.

"You look the part. You discipline well. You know the game. You've got the goods. Now get your signals crisp and rules memorized. Don't look for college games. You have no bad habits, and I don't want to see you change anything. Do women's games, CBA (Continental Basketball Association) League games. I already told Garrison about you and he's going to want to see you work."

Cecil was a Ronnie Nunn cheerleader, and Ronnie kept reaching for that gold ring.

I ran the house, attending to chores, managing finances, and of course, raising the girls. We carried full plates but kept eyes on the prizes: jobs we loved, and a comfortable home to raise our girls.

By June 1984, using savings, we purchased a raised ranch on one acre of land in Danbury, Connecticut. Knowing this unique community celebrated socioeconomic and racial diversity, offered affordable, safe housing and was a reasonable distance from our New York roots, we took a chance. Ronnie's main job, teaching special needs students in Pleasantville, was now a forty-five-minute commute that was doable. Ironically, the consideration of easing his ride didn't last very long. Ronnie's referee expertise afforded him invitations for NBA tryout camps and after traveling to Chicago and California for evaluation, he knew this opportunity was special and a credible goal. Despite pressures to bring his A game, six weeks after settling in our new home, a few years after his first officiating experience, the phone rang.

"Ronnie, good morning. It's Darrel. I'd like to offer you a position with our staff. The league office will send the contract for you to sign and return asap. You need to fill out the health care stuff and get that back to us as well. All info will be included in the overnight package. Congratulations. See you in camp."

Short and simple, Ronnie was in the league! The correspondence was from Darrel Garretson, NBA director of officiating. Out grocery shopping when I returned, my husband helped with the bags and announced, "Darrel called. Camp starts in a couple of weeks."

He sounded cool but I knew otherwise. As I listened intently, he informed me that he accepted a position as NBA referee. Finally, his dream to be part of the professional sports world came true though entering through a different doorway. I think I screamed, scaring the girls, but then hugged him tightly. "Oh my God! You did it!"

He was calm though I know proudly bursting inside. We called our parents and my sister before talking about the new particulars in our lives. We had relocated to Connecticut one month prior and the new job would take him traveling back to the Bronx, to LaGuardia Airport, to twenty-seven new cities and many days absent from home. We belie-ved the position was worth taking even though it initially decreased his salary, an issue to resolve now that a home mortgage added to our burdens. Thrilled by his impressive title, we were shocked by his wages, as the first contract severely diminished our monthly earnings. As well as losing about $10,000 a year, he owed the union $2,000 a year in dues as they collaborated with bosses for raises and perks. Colleagues assured Ronnie that every three years, contract totals bumped up significantly and he would soon be more financially secure.

We managed, never struggled, but to assure our financial security because I was a worry wart, I monitored spending, prepared macaroni, or grilled cheese often and had no problem filling our stomachs resour-cefully. We elected to receive the salary over a six-month year, knowing we could scrimp and save to meet mortgage payments. The season for new officials ended in April so additional employment during the five months off working during playoff time and throughout the summer could fill the gaps. Ronnie assured me that contracts changed every three years and eventually, we would be out of the hole. We hoped off-season jobs could replenish the deficit and refill the decreasing bank account, as well as keep me home.

I adjusted to life with a traveling man gone almost twenty days a month, but who called daily regardless of time changes and monitored his family from a distance. I filled my days now loving motherhood and a flair for the creative blossomed. Throughout the pre-school and school years, I introduced the girls to the arts. They finger-painted (something my mother never allowed because of the mess it caused), filled molds in ceramics classes, pasted gooey papier mâché masks to ease the fears associated with Halloween, and colored both inside and outside of the lines.

They studied piano, a feat Ilana mastered but Alexi rejected. Accompanied by a metronome to stop her from rushing through songs, she hated daily practicing and yearly competitions, so eventually, she quit and never touched the keys again. Ilana, on the other hand, still can tickle the ivories and enjoy time at the piano she purchased for her own home. Both soared in dance classes: ballet, jazz and tap where glittering costumes lured them to perform. They loved the stage and took part in local plays. Acting became second nature. Music filled our home as they sang lyrics with Stevie Wonder, Al Jarreau, the Jets, and the Jacksons.

We flourished and anticipated special times when Daddy returned. They gazed impatiently out the living room window, searching for the airport car to turn into the driveway.

"Daddy's home!" they shouted and jumped up and down.

They stood as he opened his suitcase and distributed small trinkets from different arenas. Stuffed gorillas from the Phoenix Suns, the San Antonio coyotes, and other mascots typically distributed favors at games and my girls were delighted. They also anticipated playing their special Barbie game in which Ronnie and doll Ken partnered. Together, they questioned the forty-one dolls in the basement play area each representing a different state, wearing a labeled banner in the girls' special Miss America pageant. That is how they mastered the country's states. Ronnie, yawning, suffering from jet lag, had to remember to alternate winners and make sure both daughters' dolls became finalists, but much to Alexi's chagrin, Miss Hawaii was his favorite, a doll belonging to Ilana.

"It's not fair! Daddy always picks Miko! I never win!" Alexi barked on a regular basis. Unfortunately, I cannot seem to locate the taped episodes of these events. No memory lane revivals.

More important, they learned to read early because the teacher in me flooded the home with books. We ventured to different worlds as the stories fostered imaginations. But one of their personal favorites was a short story about a family of rabbits where Mama continually warned, "Let Papa Sleep." They transformed into the two baby hares that could never wait for Papa to awake naturally, but rather, scurried, plotted, and found unique ways to wake him before time. As a traveling man, Ronnie tried to cheat sleep, nap whenever possible, but his little fans anxiously awaited their time with the "big tickle monster" who feigned sleep until they inched close enough to the king-sized bed and then rose with a roar, grabbed, and poked them until they could escape his grasp. Today, an aged tickle monster toys with grandchildren who mirror their parents' behavior.

There were many unique Daddy stories like watching him chase the runaway sled, girls aboard, as gravity sped it down the side of our property to be stopped by thicket and brush before hitting an oak or elm tree.

"Help!" they yelled as he tore after them.

"Are you trying to kill us?" Alexi accused. Situated in the front part of the flying sled, she now bore scratches covering his face.

Although they accused him of a type of sabotage, he convinced them to ride again and put them back on the sled to eliminate future fears.

"Come on, that's nothing. A little Neosporin or Temovate and you're as good as new!" That was his panacea for most boo-boos.

Ronnie made them laugh. They put him on a pedestal thinking he did no wrong. Anxious, they awaited every work trip return, and they reveled in his presence for a few days until he repacked and left again as they sat with sad faces pressed against the glass.

Despite the endless traveling, Ronnie, by God's grace was home during traumatic times when emergencies overwhelmed me with indecisiveness. He calmly took control when three -year -old Alexi tripped.

"Mom, Alexi is bleeding!" Ilana screamed.

Running towards the bathroom, she fell into the seam where two walls met, split her forehead, and required immediate help. I kept my wits about me and grabbed a kitchen towel holding it over the wound. Then I ran to the phone and called Ronnie at one of his parttime jobs down the street. The hero sped home, scooped her up, laid her in the car and we left for the emergency room. I was less than helpful, and the girls relied on Daddy.

"I want a plastic surgeon. It's her face," Ronnie demanded as the doctor on call examined her.

He complied and summoned a talented surgeon who informed us about how expensive but good he was before he sewed twenty-six stitches, closing Alexi's forehead. As the plastic surgeon warned she dare not move and injected Novocain into her face to repair the damage, Ronnie spontaneously invented a game: "What does Daddy do? Is he a postman? Is he a fireman? Is he a policeman or a carpenter?"

He kept her still and calm while he elicited silly responses. The shocked little girl sat motionless as the ragged tear running vertically down her forehead was mended. In the waiting area, I outwardly occupied Ilana but inwardly, I prayed.

Years later, the hero reappeared for a similar event.

"Hello Andee?" It was a neighbor calling. Ilana had left ten minutes prior to babysit for her sons. "Barkley bit Ilana! I am so sorry, but you need to get her to the emergency room."

She shared that her terrier ran at my daughter, knocking her down and unexpectedly attacked. Ronnie was home, swiftly got in the car to ride swiftly around the corner and assess the damage. I stood with Alexi in the driveway when he returned seconds later. My child held a towel across her face.

"Taking her to the hospital. You take Alexi in your car and meet us there," he instructed and sped away. *Her face!* I visualized a nip on the leg, but I was very wrong.

I learned that the frenzied dog almost tore off ten-year-old Ilana's left nostril, leaving little cartilage. Ronnie held her, reassuring her she was fine, and summoned another plastic surgeon's artistry for the repair of yet another facial wound.

"Mother needs to leave. Looks like we could lose her, and we don't want that," Doctor Goldman ordered.

The doctor deemed me useless and sent me to the waiting room to monitor Alexi and pray for good results. Deja vu.

Over the many years, Ronnie came to their aid especially while I remained paralyzed by fear. And his steady assistance continued no matter how young or grown they became. Years later, after graduating law school and in need of a vacation before work responsibilities began, Alexi selected for venture to South America with a roommate. She even talked about boats down the Amazon River, which confused me since she easily terrified if confronted with the smallest of spiders. We said nothing and sanctioned her trip.

One night, soon after, we received an unexpected call from Ecuador. It was Alexi. Not even a hello for me. "I need Daddy," she said with urgency.

I handed him the phone and watched his face redden. She had booked a tour with a law school friend but discovered that they were the only passengers. At the airport, two men representing the tour company carrying what appeared to be valid credentials greeted them. The four traveled by Ecuador.com company van from the Quito airport to an isolated ranch in what Alexi described as a pretty remote area. Alone with these escorts, she did not feel safe, locked her room door, and called home. Alarmed by how unsettled she sounded, Ronnie called the airlines and secured tickets moving her from the secluded area to the Galapagos Islands early the following morning. She was to tell the hosts that a family emergency required her to return to the airport at once. Ronnie said little but was furious that such smart women could place themselves in a precarious position, but Hero Man solved the dilemma and saved the day.

Again, Ronnie purchased a one-way return ticket for one of Ilana's beaus to return home to Spain when Dad sensed signs of unexpected unhappiness in his firstborn. He had no problem coming to the rescue time and time again. Often, during the basketball season, he rerouted travel plans to college dormitory rooms when either daughter was in crisis mode and whisked them into his arms whenever either needed healing, comfort, or protection.

Chapter 19

SPRING 1989, I accepted a parttime position as reading specialist at Henry Abbott Vocational Technical High School when Alexi was in third grade and Ilana in sixth. The high school's calendar paralleled Danbury's elementary school schedule, so I was home with them and never missed a bus stop drop-off or pick-up.

Once again in the classroom, I challenged students to rise up academically even though in this vo-tech setting their schedules split between six-week practical courses like electricity, carpentry, air conditioning/heating, and hairdressing, and six weeks of traditional academics. The big challenge was that the rotation forced me to create units that needed to be completed in one cycle or I could lose continuity. This was my first experience working in a Danbury public school with its student body reflecting the community's unique diversity. The population though predominately Caucasian, also celebrated African American, Southeast Asian, Latino and Portuguese. Funny, I was not used to composition and the older age group, but I didn't care who filled the chairs if I could get them to become accountable students and future productive citizens in my town.

Most students were blue-collar and career-focused with a rare few college-bound. Although older students could be intimidating, Connecticut was not New York, and my training proved to be a definite advantage when the kids generally believed the lady with the New York accent seemed "cool". As always, acting secure and seasoned, I managed to lure them in and attract them with creative storytelling and reading lessons to coincide.

"You need to be able to read your work manuals. You can't just rely on diagrams. Don't come to my house to fix a pipe or add an electrical outlet and not know what you're doing!

Don't think I would pay any of you if the job isn't done right."

I tried to echo voices of clients and concerns they could face. A few Saturdays, I showed up at the hairdressing department salon where apprentices practiced cutting and coloring hair usually for senior citizens attracted by lower costs and brought my daughters in for trims. They knew I was serious and rooted for their successes.

A most memorable story involved a tenth grader whose polite behavior was sometimes masked by her loudness. Yet she worked efficiently, communicated with peers, and seemed to be progressing—at least I assumed this to be the case. One spring afternoon, after a day of her absence, her panic-stricken mother called school requesting to speak with me. In an endless stream of words, she related the news. "Miss Nunn, you're not going to believe what happened. I spent all last night in the emergency room with T."

"Is she okay?" I had no idea where this was going.

"Well, I knew she was constipated and yelling in pain, so I took her for help. I figured they'd do something at Danbury Hospital. Miss Nunn, she was pregnant! She hid it from me and now we got a baby girl! But she never told me, I can't believe it. My head's scrambling. They'll be home in a few days, and I got nothing. And she's worried about school, losing credit. Told me to tell you first, oh my god!"

Trying to decipher her rambling, I realized that "T" hid a pregnancy for nine months under over-sized flannel shirts. Now she gave birth to a healthy baby girl without any prior preparation: no crib, no clothes, no diapers, no formula, no prenatal care!

"As long as everyone is healthy. We will figure this out. Let me see what I can do, and I will get back to you. Stay strong." I tried to keep her calm as my mind raced for solutions.

After picking up my girls, shopping commenced at the local Babies "R" Us store. We filled a wagon with some essentials: a few onesies, blankets, booties, caps, bibs. With some financial help from a concerned neighbor who met me in the Pampers' aisle and noticed how frenzied I appeared, I purchased a carton of diapers, lotions, wipes, and a few baby bottles to prepare the distraught grandma for the daughter and unexpected grandbaby's homecoming. I checked out a second-hand shop and found a reasonably priced used crib. Then I made a call.

"Cindy, can you meet me at your home? I gathered some supplies."

"I'm on my way, but her brother is home if you get there first. I want to kill that girl. How could I be so stupid or busy and not know?"

It took a while to regain sanity, but the family worked together and though a difficult journey, they did well. (Years later, the baby attended Danbury High while I taught there.)

Because I worked parttime, I spent fewer hours with my students, but I never forgot them. As a new teacher to the Connecticut system, multiple observation reports were required from state-appointed persons who monitored my work. Reciprocity was iffy since my degrees were not in reading, so the state system insisted I pass a set of observations. The first two were a cinch and I scored "exceptional" in every area. One more to go and I was set.

During the final observation with a state rep sitting in the last row, last seat, I was impressed that student participation, hands waving in the air continuously, reinforcing my ability to engage all in a reading lesson. One student kept summoning me to his desk, urging me to listen to his whispers.

When I approached, he whispered under his breath. "We got your back. No worries, nobody's going to give you up," he laughed.

My puzzled pause encouraged him to continue.

"We know the answers because you taught this story yesterday… wrong class, Miss, but not a problem!" I gulped and smiled gratefully.

Knowing that students behaved as they chose to either sabotage or support a teacher during any observation, I was indebted and flattered by their support. By the way, it was nerves, not the lack of lesson planning that caused my confusion that day, a mistake *never* to be repeated.

The following morning before class, I stopped at McDonald's and brought a yummy aroma into the room.

"French fries," I beamed. For their support, I rewarded their always hungry bellies. It was our little secret. I naturally passed the observation.

I spent three terms at Tech, but I still see many of my kids, now adults. One is a local firefighter, another works in Home Depot, a home improvement store I frequent, some fix my air conditioning system or plumbing problems and others, in the past, styled my hair, waited on me in restaurants or were members of construction crews updating my home. When I meet them working out in the gym or in the grocery store with their families, I remember their names and glow when they thank me for a fun class or good advice or for teaching them how to read and follow manual directions. We remember a prom without electrical power during a torrential rainstorm and a Halloween when no one knew who the Barbie in pink was, as I disguised myself so well!

Chapter 20

A UNIQUE OPPORTUNITY to work at Western Connecticut State University was an offer I dared not ignore. Since my goal was fulltime employment in the Connecticut public school system, I set up an appointment with Dr. Caruso, chairman of the education department. Although I held certifications in New York to teach speech or elementary education, reciprocity could not be assumed since each state had its own requirements. After Dr. Caruso evaluated my résumé and prior transcripts, he informed me that I was four courses short to receive CT certification as a reading specialist, which would widen job opportunities considerably.

The university's westside campus was located only two miles from my home, so with easy travel and a neighborhood babysitter, the decision to complete the coursework was a no-brainer. I enrolled in one night class each term during the school year. With Ronnie's refereeing season ending, he would be home late spring so I completed the two remaining classes in a June early summer session. I earned a 4.0 GPA, and, by early August, I received reading specialist grades K-12 certification.

During one of the last days in the summer session class, my professor, Dr. Joseph Cillizza, approached me before I left. "I've got an offer for you that you can't refuse." He paused and I waited. "How would you like to create an on-campus study skills laboratory offering assistance to a targeted incoming group of first- generation college students?"

That sounded like a lot for me to process, so I hesitated, and he continued.

"Before you say no, just listen. It's not fulltime. It's a twenty-hour, four-days-per-week position. I know your daughters are still young and you want to be home, so you create your schedule. I will make you director and provide two assistant teachers."

I remained silent as he continued.

"This is a brand-new position to run an innovative program, the Individualized Achievement Program. The IAP targets forty-four in-state potential freshmen. The prospective students consist of all specifically selected first -generation students: one-third African American, one-third Latinx and one-third combination of Asian and Caucasian students. They are primarily from the Danbury area with a few admitted from lower-income sections of Bridgeport, Stamford, and New Haven."

He took a breather and observed that he had my complete attention.

"The duties include monitoring an August summer school component for these students who require remediation in English before total fall matriculation. It's easy. You will oversee operations while another existing staff member teaches. I can't be there, so I need you to keep an eye out. But when fall term starts, duties will change. On the midtown campus, you will need to create a lab where students will be required to attend and document spending a minimum of two hours a week receiving in-house assistance. We'll provide computers, tables and it will be your home base. I've already reserved extra space, a double-size classroom. I'll provide two assistants and you can juggle hours but keep the lab open from let's say nine-to-five and add one or two later nights. Typically, less students use services in early morning. They either attend classes or sleep. The lab will be a home base for them to get help with writing /researching a paper or breaking down complex reading assignments."

Before I could ask a question, he bombarded me with more information. "You will also assume the position of course lecturer teaching a night course of study skills, two sections, each meeting once per week for two hours. You develop the curriculum. Enrollees earn two credits, and the lecturer position is in addition to an hourly salary rate for the lab."

"Sounds a bit overwhelming," I responded, with all the details swirling around my head.

"Look, each student needs a stronger skillset. In the course, you teach time management strategies like creating to-do lists, managing due dates, prioritizing assignments, and scheduling workloads. They need reading improvement: building comprehension, making inferences and other higher order skills. From reading their application essays, I see that most writing is substandard and in need of crafting thesis statements, developing outlines and writing organized paragraphs. They will attend your night class, your lab, as well as the on-campus writing lab, but they need basics in organizing their lives away from home and writing effective essays. It's like tutoring. Consider them glorified high schoolers."

When I still didn't accept, he continued with increased passion, "You're underpaid at Tech working twelve hours a week. I am offering a small initial stipend to oversee the four-week August program. Then I will double your pay for the lab, but this is still a parttime position. You will be paid as lecturer for the night work for the fall semester as well. Here, I wrote it all down. If you're interested, you need to go to the human resources office and get paperwork underway. I'm making you an offer you can't refuse!" he insisted.

Although shocked and overwhelmed, the proposition was tempting. Aside from better compensation, I was intrigued by the prospect of teaching college. I did not pause for too long. I could make the hours work. Running the lab position and overseeing the summer components didn't worry me, but I also needed time to develop a curriculum outline for the night course.

"It's a large undertaking, a major transition. I need to consider the work and whether I can accomplish what is necessary in your timeframe. Also, I want to discuss this with my husband before accepting your offer. Can I call you in a day or two?"

He agreed and I left, knowing I really didn't need time. Ronnie agreed that I should jump at this opportunity. I did not fathom how much I would love the university setting, the job, and the young people who I could see firsthand.

I was working with young adults ranging from eighteen through twenty-two who acknowledged that this opportunity afforded them a college education only if they committed to the initial summer program stipulations and earned passing grades. A few tested the waters, lost the chance, and were swiftly removed from the program during the summer session. Reasons for dismissal varied from illegal drinking, smuggling kegs of beer into dormitories, inappropriate behavior, breaking curfews or simply the failure to complete assignments and take responsibility. Some did not meet the bare minimal requirements of passing remedial classes in both English and math. Those individuals had decided to party too hardy, enjoyed the new dorm life independence and prioritized making love connections rather than achieving academic progress. But the majority fared well.

Potential students on the waiting list filtered into the program eagerly and forty-four matriculated for fall semester. The rest of the student body never recognized the unique forty-four and their special admittance because we avoided labels to eliminate stigmas. All carried at least twelve credits and followed mandatory guidelines attending a minimum of two hours per week in my lab, as well as one night a week in whichever session worked in a student's schedule. I taught both.

Soon, my study skills laboratory became a welcoming place where students mastered new methods to break down complex concepts, developed well-written, grammatically correct essays with provable theses and eliminated procrastination by learning time management techniques. I hired Nina, a brilliant, experienced teacher to assist with English essay development and John, a spry graduate student to cover history assignments. Math and science were not part of our duties since those departments offered their own tutorials.

The female assistant, initially all business, soon learned that emotional connections were also necessary for success in this lab. Encouragement and positive reinforcement accompanied instruction. The enthusiastic male employee, a recent graduate, was familiar with student life on campus. He embraced our students and demonstrated positivity. John was flexible and agreed to the later-hour schedule for those who claimed to focus more easily right before or after dinner. The team juggled availability and remained together all three years.

I witnessed the first IAP class become better learners, some of whom eventually I hired and worked alongside me to assist their peers. Eager to earn a stipend and raise their status, three students filled the positions after their first successful year. Because the lab attendance continued to grow and students returned even when no longer required to do so, the administration offered stipends for student hires. Every summer, a new group entered the program and the lab population swelled from our initial forty-four students to 132 walk-ins who heard about our special lab.

Students from diverse ethnic and socioeconomic backgrounds filled the lab where they felt a sense of belonging, but there was one commonality they all shared: All first-generation students, the family's first college students were ready and hungry to grab America's gold ring, a bachelor's degree. Their stories fill my head and I smile remembering them. Later, news of the lab's success spread and others on campus joined. It became a home base for many, mostly students of color, who felt a sense of belonging.

Throughout this narrative, I intend to share stories about impact they had on my teaching, on my life. Knowing them brought the realization that their bodies did not simply fill empty seats in my classroom. Their backgrounds and needs differed by socioeconomic status, ethnicity, race, religion, and gender identification, but they shared common goals: gain knowledge and feel respected. Each uniquely molded by personal experiences, did not benefit from cookie-cutter curriculums. From them, I learned to juggle. I adapted lessons that satisfied their learning styles, satisfied their academic objectives, maintained their interest, and paralleled school guidelines.

José

During my first encounter with José, he complained about his inability to write. "I think I broke my finger, so I can't write. I can't complete the assignment, Miss."

Because he hurt his finger horsing around, he swore he couldn't use it. I heard lots of excuses, but his complaints went nowhere fast.

"Tape your wounded finger to its adjacent neighboring digit. Do you understand me? Night will end soon, it's just around the bend, and that paper is due tomorrow at 9:00."

The annoyance written on my face shut him down and even though he was mumbling under his breath, he left understanding my position. I was informed by classmates that during the wee hours off the morning, José completed his opening autobiographical piece and submitted it on time.

José's writing opened a new world for me as he shared the richness of the Dominican Republic of his youth and then, his shock of coming to America. His descriptive language painted a picture of his *isla*, where tropical fruits tempted the palate and sea breezes eased the heat's intensity. It was a home to remember when the family divided. Mother and sons moved to the Pennsylvania and later, to New York living in small, shabby apartments he yearned to forget. His words stung with the injury of abandonment and prejudice as the innocent boy questioned the loss of a male role model, life's unfair treatment and his feelings of powerlessness on foreign soil. I read of his school experiences and class placements in America that left him unchallenged and frankly, bored.

By the time his mother relocated her boys to Danbury, José felt no incentives to learn, became a class clown, which reinforced the negative image of many immigrant boys who mistakenly appeared uninvolved rather than overwhelmed by new surroundings. He failed courses. No educator uncovered his inquisitive nature, his love of history and the History Channel, and the wealth of information he possessed but never shared in the lowest level, tracked classes. He yearned for advanced placement offerings, dared to challenge himself, but was denied access because of his academic record. Barely graduating with his class and left with no direction, he wandered hopelessly until he learned of the new IAP program.

"I got accepted because of drugs. Some clown didn't follow the rules and got thrown out. So, I took his place," José bragged.

After two years of earning top grades and building his grade point average without further excuses, he joined my lab's staff as a student assistant until he graduated with honors. His welcoming personality and ability to encourage peers made him an asset to my small group of student teachers/mentors and added financial assistance to his empty pockets. He often bragged that his empty pockets would soon be filled knowing that higher education opens new avenues and better earning power.

Before long, as a certified history teacher, José shared his knowledge and reached deeply into struggling communities, offering education as a solution to ease socioeconomic issues. Today, he holds three degrees. At the Bridges Academy, a charter school in Bridgeport, Connecticut, he served as history chairperson where he boasted of 100% enrollment in college by his graduates. He has also served as adjunct professor at Quinnipiac College where he instructed future teachers and impacts the next generation of educators.

As of this writing, he is a leader of our Latino community who challenges our system, accusing schools of failing our ESL population. He is raising funds and fighting to start a charter school in our community. He and his colleagues proudly opened and christened LEAD (Latinos for Educational Advocacy and Diversity), a community center mainly to service our Danbury Latinx population but opened to all.

Working with José taught me never to give up on students that initially appear unmotivated. He changed my predisposed opinion regarding students that seem disinterested but are uncertain of their potential. They often need a mentor whose elixir combines direction and nurturing.

Sonia

Sonia meekly entered the lab one day searching for assistance with writing an English essay. Although she understood the course material, she floundered, unsure of how to write an effective, provable hypothesis. She sat down at an available computer, spent endless minutes staring at the screen, began typing, but was too shy to ask for direction. Normally, my staff and I never wanted to appear too anxious or overbearing like salespersons on commission, so we waited for students to summon us, explain their needs and then we would proceed with direction. This young lady looked over her shoulder but couldn't utter a sound.

Later that morning, I eased a rolling chair beside her. "Hi, I'm Mrs. Nunn. Need me or Mrs. B to look over something?"

Sonia lit up and nodded. She needed tutorial help, yearned to be more proficient, needed reassurance. After that isolated incident, Sonia became a fixture in the lab. With a voracious appetite to learn, she often was the first to arrive and the last to leave.

I discovered that Sonia was a Danbury High graduate gifted with artistic talent. Her goal was to teach art in our community and become a role model for young Dominican women. Strong traditions from the old country routed girls to marry early, not pursue higher education, but rather, work as homemakers, mothers, and wives. Sonia, the fourth child, second girl to go to college, defied the norms, understood the importance of higher learning, and did not bring grandbabies into the family as expected. She later earned a bachelor's degree and state certification to teach art. Yet, despite her accomplishments, she underestimated her ability and still struggled with completion of a final thesis for the sixty credit the MFA degree she pursued.

Along the way, she became an integral part of my family, babysat for my daughters, and participated in family gatherings. As a young adult she traveled with me as we ventured to Rome and Florence, Italy to visit my daughter studying abroad. Who better to explore the art experience of the Uffizi Museum, the wonders of the Sistine Chapel and the magnificence of David, a statue that took my breath away, something that had not happened to me since seeing my husband that first day in the school hallway. Sonia became my personal guide explaining the masters' techniques and styles throughout the journey.

All was fine until the return trip to the States. Security ignored everyone ahead of us and everyone behind us as travelers passed through the checkpoints, but they focused on my brown-skinned, curly-haired companion. "Please step out of the line."

The guard pointed and directed her to stand behind an opaque screen where she was soon joined by a female agent. Of course, Sonia obeyed orders. Frustrated by the lengthy body search she faced before being excused and on her way, she remarked, "Well, that was degrading,"

The attitude towards minorities changed after the 9/11 attacks and overly cautious customs' guards were weary of anyone who could pass as a person of Middle Eastern descent. Sonia shared that being singled out was not a new experience and she just dealt with it as an uncomfortable inconvenience. We snickered, thinking that she certainly didn't appear threatening and there was no indication of wrongdoing, but we both knew how stereotypes flourish and although aggravated, we followed procedures and dealt with the security issues.

For years, Sonia has been an elementary school art teacher in Darien, Connecticut where she proffers her talent and offers a cultural richness to a town historically not known for its openness to diversity. Ironically, a teaching position never opened for her in hometown Danbury, a perfect fit because initially administrators wanted her to fill in for an ESL educator on leave, but she did not feel qualified for that job even though it might have led to fulltime art instruction. So, the opportunity to work in her hometown disappeared. Yet she works to unlock closed minds and enrich the art program wherever she goes. We talk and meet occasionally usually when she stops by with some unique lunch goodies to share. We talk of future endeavors, and I laugh about how we aged. Time never stops and during our friendship, I taught her twenty-year-old niece first at Danbury High and again at the university.

It was not until twenty years after our meeting that I learned of the adversity Sonia faced as a child. With unresolved angst, she shared childhood experiences when she was often berated rather than nurtured. She shared that her self-worth and self-confidence were robbed from her as a child and the trauma she faced daily morphed her into an insecure child who battled a speech disorder, a stutter that plagued her for years. Sonia confessed that her parents were victims of extreme poverty. Their large, struggling family and old-world rules did not allow them to see new opportunities for their daughters in this country. The two older sisters were rebellious role models who broke the mold, sought higher education, and demonstrated that being baby-making homemakers was not their main life purpose. They opened new doors and Sonia finally felt empowered to make her mark as an education, but when her beloved older sister died unexpectedly, inconsolable, Sonia hoped for bonding closer with her parents. Yet despite the tragedy that befell the family, she saw little change in family dynamics and learned to acknowledge that the approval she sought would not suddenly appear. The loss was overwhelming, but she learned to focus her eyes on her craft. She persevered.

Taking the road not expected is not an easy task. Understanding Sonia's plight helped me support other young women like her, particularly from the Latinx community, who wanted to pursue careers other than homemaker. Through scholarships and incentives, many received certifications and/or degrees in a variety of fields.

STEVE

Steve joined the lab family and sat at a computer adapted with programs to facilitate his learning. Legally blind, he required assistance and needed materials enlarged for him. Yet, Steve's upbeat personality never permitted him to wallow in self-pity or make excuses for his never-ending challenges. As a member of the IAP program, he intended to pursue a career in meteorology, his passion. Part of his daily routine included a recitation of present weather conditions across the state and an in-depth explanation of future patterns and pending conditions to monitor. With his nose literally against the monitor, Steve read assignments and attempted to decipher them and take notes. Often, I read material to him, studied orally with him knowing that repetition eased his studying. Writing notes and reading texts were arduous tasks without adaptations. A few professors felt irritated with the time needed to make adjustments for him in a timely manner.

Although the law mandates that adjustments be made for visually impaired students, some of his meteorology teachers were not in compliance. A handful did not complete adjustments in a timely manner or wish to add duties to their filled days. I attempted to enlarge maps and charts to remedy the situation, but for Steven the work became overwhelming and department members discouraged his pursuit.

"I think I need to change majors. I love weather but I can't keep up," a frustrated Steven remarked.

"Why not try communications? With your engaging personality it could be a great fit?" I suggested.

After numerous discussions, I persuaded Steve to switch majors and keep the study of weather as a hobby rather than the chore he had begun to resent. As a new communications major, Steve's charisma added to his course presentations, speeches, and group dynamics and he was seemingly content.

And then he faced another challenge. Despite my objections, a PE department representative insisted Steve participate in a gym course without understanding that group sports did not work for this student. Eventually we resolved this painstaking issue with a unique solution: a walking class; Steven signed in and then three hours per week, walked unescorted on and off campus.

When he did not arrive at the lab for his scheduled appointment one morning as expected, I panicked, began walking and searching the campus. I discovered that Steven, filling his gym requirement, walked too far, and got lost. I found him in the adjacent cemetery after he mistakenly turned left, which took him off campus grounds.

"I guess I made a wrong turn! Got a little shook. I have no clue where I am. I am just glad you found me!"

Mulling over the dilemma, I remedied the problem by finding alternating volunteers to walk with him and ease his tension. After all, he had the gift of gab and could entertain whoever accompanied him as he filled the gym requirement to graduate.

"Hmm, what's that yummy smell? Are we eating?" he laughed as he entered the lab one morning.

He often bragged about how his upbringing in an Italian home afforded him the ability to distinguish aromas in the kitchen. I warmed food in the room's microwave, and I couldn't sneak a snack because Steve's keen sense of smell could distinguish between pretzels and chips, forcing me to share. Hearing the crunch or smelling an aroma, Steve left me with two choices: either eat on the sly or be willing to open the bag and share my food.

"Love the new pictures of you! Adds interest to the walls," he remarked casually one morning.

I laughed when he walked up to newly added motivational posters, face to the wall, complimenting the great new pictures of me.

"Steven, that one is Oprah Winfrey, and the other, Mahatma Gandhi! I am highly insulted!"

He saw no color, had no peripheral vision, viewed the world differently, but loved learning and offered a sense of innocence and sincere friendship to all of us. He simply chuckled when I corrected him. "Oops, sorry."

Steve's passion included strong adoration for Donna Summer's music. He memorized lyrics to every song and was an active fan club member. "I know I will never meet her, but I can wish," he chuckled.

In 2015, on his Facebook page, I discovered that at a social event, he made history when he entertained as part of a special performance. With a strong partner, he danced to Summer's "Last Dance", and completed one of his earlier "to do-list" wishes. And years later, he met Donna Summer at a concert and posed for a remembrance photo.

After he earned his degree, Steve was first hired by an optical company working to improve products and programs for visually impaired usage. A few years later, he purchased a condominium and chose to ease his challenges by getting a guide dog to help him venture through life. Because he was so likeable, his neighbors helped him navigate icy steps, directed him towards the bus and kept a watchful eye out for this special, young man.

A few years later, he was hired by Oak Hill School for the blind where he taught others how to use available digital programs. His statewide presentations continued to bring awareness to others and advocate for adaptations. He was an avid meteorology and weather aficionado who posted up-to-date weather patterns, followed storms, and found fascination in climate issues. He once commented: "Top100! #24. Eva, OK April 15, 2016. This supercell dropped several tornadoes with this being the first! Fantastic day! At one point there were two white tornadoes side by side from our vantage point."

I pictured him, nose to the enlarged images loving every minute of his weather clips listening to Donna Summer music playing in the background. Steve exhibited an inner drive that allowed him to see beyond his blindness. I learned limitations did not have to railroad students; they just needed detours to find the finish line and live contented lives.

In November 2022, tragically, while walking on the Oak Hill school campus grounds during the early morning, Steven and his partner were struck by a reckless, speeding driver. Both were instantly killed. The tributes written in memory demonstrated how his warm spirit and effervescence filled so many. My heart hurt that day.

KEVIN

Kevin's cool persona and guarded body language left little chance for connections with peers. His knowledge of both African American and Black history, along with his personal past experiences, left him leery of teachers who look like me. He carried his mistrust and hesitancy into my laboratory where his presence was mandated according to program guidelines. Although those accepted into the IAP were required to spend a minimum two to three hours a week in my lab for tutorial assistance, for months, he simply observed and isolated himself behind a computer typing. Kevin sat in silence, began writing and eventually shared a piece of original poetry with me hoping I would act as his personal spell checker. His phonetic spellings were easily corrected, but his words sang, and his images lifted off the computer paper and danced in my head. I read brilliance in Kevin's word mastery and couldn't hide my excitement.

"You like?"

When he realized that I got it, he thawed and kept returning to the lab sharing his pieces, earning praise and acknowledgement, as well as accepting constructive criticism. We developed a mentor/mentee relationship.

He, a great debater, always ready for a verbal argument, challenged the government policies regarding education, economics and race and sought to reveal and erase institutional racism. He emerged as a radical voice on campus. But his posturing scared many until he slightly eased his aggressive style and although hesitant with white folk, he engaged some and looked beyond skin tone. Always weary, he carefully selected conversations yet was never afraid to confront anyone he did not trust.

After year one, I hired him to assist as a student tutor. With deliberate patience and eloquence, he explained lessons and encouraged peers to work. At first, his stoic ways scared many who sought help but soon reassured visitors that he was there to offer his knowledge despite working without a smile. Kevin officially morphed into one of the lab rats who bonded together to reach the stars.

He earned his degree, left campus initially returning to his hometown, Stamford, but joined me for a few lunches. I watched him glow as he shared the news about expecting a son and understanding the new responsibilities would be never-ending. For a long while we lost touch, but he continues to fight for equity. After teaching history in Las Vegas and raising a strong son, Kevin returned to Connecticut.

Although we rarely see one another, we are lifelong friends. He calls me on Mother's Day and reminisces about the past, as well as complains about the present and loses hope in the future. Kevin, a single father, taught his son about the reality of being a young Black man in a country that often stereotypes young men like him. In an atmosphere of uncertainty, Kevin shares the past plight of civil rights workers trying to right the wrongs, as well as the current police brutality and countless murdering of men of color. Although with the election of Barack Obama, new heights seemed possible, when he stepped down and the baton was handed to a president and cabinet less than open-minded, Kevin talked the talk and prepared his son with martial arts experience, as well as education. The surge in racism, anti-Semitism and inequities reinforce his attitude of faithlessness.

For many, men like Kevin are intimidating. With his mastery of words, knowledge of political issues and outward boldness, he scared many. His passion was real, his concerns real and his voice echoed raw honesty, truth that made others feel uneasy. I learned that racism in this country has a historic past and a presence today as well. I listened, making certain he could back his claims with facts to win arguments and I brought that idea to others in my room.

CHANTHIP

Another memorable young woman sat in the laboratory typing her archetypal journey, sharing an incredible family history that began in Cambodia. She enlightened me about how her life was shaped by the trials and tribulations of poverty, sexism, and war. Her words echoed the millions whose world turned upside down because of the Khmer Rouge takeover that forced her family's migration to America.

Quiet, unassuming Chanthip eventually met a South African young man who migrated here for a better life. As a "colored" from his native country, he dealt with Apartheid and its consequences. Fortunately, Judge West from Danbury who previously relocated his sister, Carla, to our town, now sponsored the young man and brought him here, as well. He witnessed both racial and socioeconomic diversity in Danbury and began studies along with his sister who attended Western at the time. Carla introduced him to Chanthip and immediately, the pair bonded. However, new family objections sparked as Chanthip battled her mother's threats about dating outside her Southeast Asian community. Outwardly she demonstrated obedience as she quietly continued attending classes but in a short time, she married her young man despite the family's disapproval.

In 2013, about twenty years after she attended sessions my college lab, her firstborn child, a daughter, Jasmine, occupied a seat in my American Studies high school class. Not until she shared her story, did I realize who she was and what had happened to the reserved woman who raised her.

Jasmine

Jasmine sat in American Studies class soaking in information but rarely engaging in discussions. Yet, her assignments demonstrated total understanding of the complex concepts covered in a course that integrated American history and English throughout the decades. Although the fifty students enrolled usually worked in groups of four to five, Jasmine's strong writing skills and evident artistic talent set her apart, allowing her to shine.

At Danbury High in our multicultural environment, I was surrounded by a sea of difference. Students from all over the globe speaking about forty different languages often shared their stories and cultural backgrounds. Jasmine's unique blended background resulted in exceptional beauty that she downplayed. Dressing in a simplistic style and wearing no make-up was not typical of many eleventh-grade females who often posed peacock-style to attract the attention of young men seeking teenage relationships. She appeared uninterested, keeping to herself. And then one day she revealed her story in an assigned autobiographical sketch which ironically, caused flashbacks in my life.

Although Jasmine, a native Connecticut Yankee, was born in Danbury, neither of her parents shared her roots. Her mother, Chanthip, along with her family, fled from Cambodia after the Khmer Rouge occupied their homeland. They were called "the boat people" who resettled in America seeking new freedoms. Somehow, Danbury became a haven and youngsters with Americanized names tried to assimilate and recover from the chaos occurring in Southeast Asia. Struggling with language, weather, and new culture, they understood the sacrifices made by parents who burdened them with pressures of school performance and household responsibilities. Parents worked too many hours and expected their children to grab the American Dream while juggling their responsibilities. Education here was a privilege previously denied and there were no options but academic success. Children were obligated to succeed and then take on the responsibilities of caring for aging parents. Youngsters evolved into adults carrying burdens that included guilt of parent struggles and sacrifices.

Jasmine's mother, Chanthip, attempted to be the obedient daughter. In high school, she maintained excellent grades and continued her role as a dutiful daughter who completed assigned household chores and assisted with raising siblings. Eventually, her dedication to learning earned her admission to Western Connecticut State University where she entered the nursing program. I met her in 1990 when she walked into my study skills laboratory where, as a member of an individualized academic program, she received assistance with writing and language skills when needed. She plowed through assignments successfully until a detour blocked her path. Chanthip befriended a lovely classmate, Caulda Jacobs, and their special bond blossomed. And then Caulda's brother, a handsome, tall man with golden complexion, entered the picture. Smitten with each other, Chanthip and the young man pushed cultural differences aside and became a couple. Although Chanthip attempted to keep the relationship a secret, family troubles began almost immediately.

The Jacobs children were transported to America by Judge West, a prominent African American who mentored them and welcomed them to Danbury. Born in Apartheid-driven South Africa, they were classified as "colored" in the caste system that governed their country and limited their potential. Here they, too, could reach for the gold ring and follow the American Dream.

Chanthip's alarmed parents rejected the new boyfriend and did not sanction the marriage. She was expected to bring a Cambodian boy into the family rather than this foreigner from a different race. Going against her parents initially severed family ties, but Chanthip's determination and adoration moved her towards the unwelcomed union. Hostilities permeated the couple's first years, but they carried the burdens and marched to their own drummer. Education on hold, they created a family and juggled numerous jobs to keep the home stable. Against all odds, their love overpowered obstacles and the marriage survived.

Hardened hearts softened when children were born, and Jasmine was the first child!

Jasmine shared that Chanthip bore eight babies and finally returned to school to earn her degree. The family remains united despite the objections they faced. And here, in my classroom, sat the product of their strong love.

Jasmine made her mark in a large class of fifty students. Although she rarely volunteered her thoughts during class conversations, her brilliantly written pieces always screamed her opinions. Whether creating passionate poetry to describe a historic event or sketching her ideas with pen and ink renderings, Jasmine offered an honest reaction supported by facts and beautiful artwork.

I later learned that this talented young woman also excelled in the sciences with the intention of entering the biology field in college. She entered Western, maintained parttime employment, and still assisted in raising the younger brood at home. Her appearance altered as she explored piercing, dying her hair in neon colors and searching for her identity. Still focused on her education, I recently met her working retail in our local mall where we embraced. I encouraged her to continue writing even though her scientific expertise is her focus.

From Chanthip, I learned that many of my Southeast students felt enormous pressures from family to pursue the American Dream flawlessly. No time for socialization or play. Here to learn, prosper economically and harden oneself to the burdens of the past. I saw them in my room as they honored family without complaining. I respected them and directed them as I could, trying to ease the heavy loads they carried.

Chapter 21

ALTHOUGH I LOVED working as director of the study skills lab at Western, administration never offered me full-time employment. I received small yearly raises but admittedly, I wanted the benefits and title that were associated with fulltime work schedules. I thought I earned the promotion, and many fought for me to stay, but nothing changed.

By 1994, I aimed for a teaching position in Danbury with teachers' hours to correspond with my daughters' schedules. The girls were attending full-day local public school and were comfortable riding the school bus together and meeting me at home. When in August, I learned that the Danbury schools posted openings and needed reading teachers in both middle schools, Broadview and Rogers Park, I scheduled an interview to meet with the principals. Either could individually decide whether I was a viable candidate for their school. Both jobs included medical benefits and retirement plans that were enticing. With ten years' teaching experience in Brooklyn, a short stint at the local Henry Abbott Technical High School and my three years at Western, I was certain to be considered a viable candidate.

At that time the Nunn name was familiar in our community because of Ronnie's NBA affiliation in the sports world and my daughters' academic successes and extracurricular activity involvement. For those reasons, I believe the interviewers greeted me with some enthusiasm.

As I entered the room, one principal opened the conversation. "Are you Ronnie Nunn's wife? The NBA official?"

Although I was used to this, I was in my comfort zone now, so I responded in a kidding but respectful manner, "I'm Andee Nunn, Ronnie is my husband."

Name out of the way, my résumé delineated plenty of prior experience. After about an hour, I politely shook hands, said goodbyes, and was told I would be notified in a couple of days about the decision. Although I tend to get nervous selling my worth, I felt confident that the meeting went well.

Surprisingly, later that same afternoon as I entered my home, the house phone rang. The school district's head of personnel introduced himself. "Good afternoon, Andee. Jay Enriquez here. I am pleased to offer you a position as reading specialist at Rogers Park Middle School under Principal Spielberg."

Before I could accept, he continued, "Unfortunately, we have a restricted budget, so I can't offer you a salary commensurate with your years of experience, but the position includes all health benefits and a yearly salary higher than the basic entrance level because we value your expertise. We would love having you join us. Interviews are on-going, so we ask for your response sooner than later."

I did not hesitate. I was excited! This opportunity was a gateway into public school. The job offer gave me a schedule that coincided with my daughters' obligations, worked with my parenting responsibilities, supplied the extras I wanted and would use my knowledge.

"Mr. Enriquez, I believe this is a perfect fit for me. I would like to discuss this with my family and contact you tomorrow morning. Thank you for the offer."

Ronnie agreed that this was a no-brainer for me. The following morning, I accepted the position, traveled to the local Board of Education administration offices where I signed my contract and was given a full description about my responsibilities.

My ten years in Brooklyn seasoned me and there were almost no discipline issues that I couldn't handle. Problems or glitches were minor, and I thrived. I loved the kids, and they loved me back. I got along with the other teachers although our styles differed tremendously. I was an enthusiastic nurturer and most of my colleagues were experienced veterans, yet the atmosphere in my room appeared friendlier than my colleagues. Some students said when they left the classes on the second floor and walked one flight up to reading with Ms. Nunn, they entered heaven.

After I heard that, I would greet each class with, "Welcome to Heaven. *Nunn-better* is here!"

For six years, I enjoyed the position, greeting each new season with excitement trying to make reading enjoyment contagious. I bombarded my classes with books and even reluctant or struggling readers participated and watched their skills improve. I introduced sophisticated vocabulary using mnemonics devices and pictures to engage learners. During study halls, I ran advanced workshops for gifted students whose reading abilities required additional challenges and they proudly read high school-level stories. There were many standouts, with the first being Bruno.

A young boy, who emigrated from Brazil to America, sat in my classroom ready to learn. He understood minimal English learned in his native country before he arrived in Danbury. Always wearing a winning smile, he was ready to work, ready to absorb all I offered. Bright-eyed and anxious, he listened, questioned, and learned faster than his peers whose first language was English.

Before long, the head ESL teacher approached me and firmly suggested that the boy be transferred into his program where ESL teachers used a systematic and successful approach for immigrant learners. "One of our teachers speaks Portuguese and can teach him all subjects in his native language. It is a smarter fit for him."

But I was skeptical and initially rejected his proposal. "Sorry, I disagree. Bruno works without frustration and gobbles up information. He is constantly engaged in oral conversations practicing with English speakers in the room. I think ESL placement will slow down his progress. He is not falling behind. In fact, I think he is rightly placed, seems comfortable and is advancing rapidly. Maybe you can pull him out for science or history, but I need him here for Reading. His written and oral English and his reading text are beyond my expectations. I want him with me!"

We battled, but I did not give in. I already differentiated instruction and Bruno eagerly accepted all challenges. He agreed and refused to leave.

Bruno tore across the finish line. His reading gains were off the chart as he soared in all classes. Teachers marveled at his winning attitude, as well as his engaging personality. How was it possible for a middle school boy to be so charismatic and focused when tempted regularly by some peers who opted for socializing rather than academic achievement?

Later in high school, still wearing his unforgettable smile, his academic record continued to be impressive. Also, as a member of the high school soccer team, he exhibited talent on the field. Although he appeared a bit too lanky and possibly not strong enough, he played smart and along with one teammate, Joey Dos Santos, he earned victory after victory throughout his high school playing days.

Yet, as a senior with excellent grades, as well as athletic prowess, he had to fight for scholarships and college acknowledgement. His coach advised him to give up the sport and his father told him to forget education and pursue work since he wouldn't or couldn't pay college bills. But Bruno became his own advocate. With the same work ethic that he brought with him as a young learner, he persisted. After acceptance into Marist College, Bruno realized that the minimal financial aid package offered was not enough to send him to school without major loans.

Spending endless hours practicing and building his endurance by running and exercising, he would not give up. His younger brother, Gustavo, who later sat in my high school classroom, acted as personal goalie, and assisted him with his daily workout regime. At the onset of the fall term when teams were practicing for the upcoming semester, a determined Bruno scheduled a meeting with Marist soccer coaches and asked to walk onto their practice field to show his skills. Impressed but reluctant, the coach agreed. Not only did his persistence earn him a position on the team, but Marist also awarded an additional $7,000 a year for his team participation. That left $10,000 deficit for the year, a sum Bruno believed he would manage as his only loan.

During the season, neighboring college coaches witnessed the team player in action and offers to transfer started to fill his plate. This gave Bruno negotiating power as he marched once more into his coach's office to plead his case. "You've seen me work. You know I add to the team. You know my dedication. I need a full-ride coach, or I have to transfer. Oh, and I am running a high GPA."

No longer settling for the previous arrangement, Bruno wanted a full athletic/academic scholarship for his efforts. There was no hesitation, no argument from the staff. His three remaining years were covered completely, and his soccer career got a stamp of approval. At age twenty, he earned his BA in finance, ready for the next hurdle before him.

The reality he faced included a degree from what he labeled "mediocre" rated university to enter a finance field that selected from too many Ivy League candidates. Initially, there were no opportunities offered, no interviews granted. Doors were shut. He also knew he was a very young, brown-skinned man in a Caucasian field. At the time, mega companies rarely hired men of color except for the exceptional few from Harvard or Yale. But he knocked on doors and a manager finally gave him a chance.

It's a long story that includes a pregnant wife and minimal funds to survive. But again, Bruno was relentless in his pursuit for success. Juggling accounts, he earned money for his firm, but saw no changes in his position. When others were fired, he vied for their territory and position, but when bosses gave him the territory, it was without a title advancement or financial reward. Eventually, he approached them again, agreed to a difficult travel schedule and hopped from state to state helping company accounts to demonstrate his worth.

Finally, meeting an important in-house source who witnessed his productivity opened new doors. He earned a new opportunity, the LA territory, so he relocated his family to Redondo Beach, California.

Twenty-one years since Bruno sat in my class, he texted me and planned a visit during his short return to Connecticut with his brother and best friend, Gustavo.

We broke bread, sat at my kitchen table, and reminisced about his journey. His position was as managing director and national head of family office investment sales. He mentioned he would soon be a homeowner as well. I also learned that Gustavo was living his dream refurbishing and selling specialty cars. I recalled his off-task behavior in American Studies when he was sketching cars rather than focusing on the curriculum!

Perhaps Gustavo is the unsung hero in this story, the personal cheerleader Bruno had by his side as he climbed the ladder. A devoted brother and uncle, he supported and aided Bruno in his plight. The proud brothers sought the American Dream and made it their realities. I was so thrilled to hear all their great news.

But terrible news had filled my room when my friend and counterpart, Bob, was diagnosed with stage four terminal cancer. We had partnered since day one and built a strong bond. Our six years were filled with endless discussions, laughs and tears as we shared work obligations, as well as lives away from the building. Initially, we fought the diagnosis together, denied the prognosis and kept positive when he began chemotherapy. I supported him, helped him with school responsibilities and needs at home.

His body dwindled. With little meat left on his bones, he had trouble sleeping or finding a comfortable position. Unsettled, I coaxed his daily substitute teacher to drive me to the local Costco in his open-back truck. We found a heavily stuffed corduroy Lazy-Boy lounge and dragged it into the truck and drove directly to Bob's home. I nicknamed it the "Lazy-Bob" so he could find a position that worked better. He opened the door, shook his head in disbelief and silently let us place it in his living room facing the television. We said little, but he smiled gratefully. But, by April, he left on medical leave when treatment lessened his strength, and he could not complete the year. Bob detested going for treatment, believing his fight was useless and by June, he rejected the medical regimen and conceded. We organized his papers, considered his wishes, and involved his children before he faded away. We had provided a support system for each other, and I felt broken without him. During his absence, fearing the inevitable, my spark flickered.

I approached my chairman before we left for summer break. I knew Bob's end was approaching and I selfishly needed a change. I asked to be transferred to the high school. Too many memories of Bob in our Rogers Park office haunted me, and I hoped a new beginning might reignite my spark. Also, I would work again with many of my former students as they now attended Danbury High. We discussed the situation and he agreed to the transfer.

By the middle of July, Bob's fight ended. I wrote and delivered the eulogy for my dear friend. Never to be forgotten, always missed.

Chapter 22

IN 2000, I transferred to our local high school and would work with older teens since I remembered how successful prior years at the college were for me with a more mature audience. Thinking back, I still remembered my inability to gain fulltime employment at Western, but my move to the public schools was a good fit.

For the first time in my teaching history, I was hired under my English certification and assigned to teach three sophomore English classes and ended the day with one double period of American Studies for juniors. Classes were leveled according to student ability placements. I taught three different sophomore classes including honors, on-level and basic designed for struggling students, as well as honor junior classes, which completed my schedule. It was a lot to digest so I sought out a mentor. Rich Harris, a seasoned teacher and department leader, was approachable and guided me through the transition. I ran many ideas past him for approval before adding them to lessons. His direction helped with my decision making.

English curricula included both classic literature and modern works, but typical of my style, I also told stories. Making connections to life helped the material come alive. Whether I bragged about a personal connection to Laurence Fishburne while studying the play "Othello" or compared Author McBride's *The Color of Water* to my family experiences, I meshed work with my reality, making the literature relatable in the best way I could. When students made personal connections and were able to link information, understanding, retention and performance improved. Ironically, the mandatory Connecticut Mastery Exam instructed students to describe a personal connection to an assigned reading selection, so my style helped prepare them.

My chairman also teamed me with a history teacher to teach eleventh grade American Studies, a class that integrated American Literature and American History. After a quick introduction to one another, my new partner suggested we meet.

Who was this man who never smiled?

"We need to work together over the summer and prepare units for the fall semester. The course moves decade by decade and we use lessons that are complementary and work for both of us," he stated stoically.

I nodded.

During the summer we met weekly sitting at my kitchen table for hours designing the course. We blended history units with literature coordinating each era starting with colonial America moving towards modern times. I embarked on a journey into the unknown and began a partnership with Joe Vas, a knowledgeable historian and scholar, who, besides our course assignment, taught only AP American history classes.

The staff's consensus was we would never last.

"Oil and water!"

We were polar opposites with nothing in common. Bets were taken about how quickly the odd couple would fail. The stoic, conservative intellect, teamed with the creative, optimistic, liberal enthusiast, were certain to clash. We broke the usual mold.

Ironically, this unlikely pair became a dynamic duo whose reputation kept the classroom rosters filled year after year. We were opposites but the contrast worked, and we fed off one another. Vas cringed when I labeled him my "morning husband" and sighed each year on Character Day when I arrived dressed as his clone: white shirt, dark tie, black sweater vest, beige khakis, suede shoes and the infamous "JOE" belt with a brass buckle that advertised his name. One Christmas, I attempted to alter his accessorizing when I ordered a neon, blinking battery-operated belt that flashed, "Vas and Nunn Forever" and "History Rocks". He wore it for about ten minutes and claimed that the fastener refused to stay closed, so it ended up a keepsake in a drawer somewhere. Some days we wore the same colors coincidentally, but I announced it as a planned event to students who always believed me over him. He shook his head at my antics, rolled his eyes and coped with my silliness. The balance between us just worked: George and Gracie, Dezi, and Lucy, Joe, and Andee.

On a more serious note, he taught me more history than my college professors and together, we developed a challenging curriculum that kept young people interested and thinking critically. With my speech and theater background, I integrated public speaking, drama, role-playing, video production and open mic poetry recitations that made assignments more creative. He brought facts, logic and understanding to every decade we examined. I think he learned to nurture from the nurturer as I gained substantial knowledge about this nation's past by analyzing numerous viewpoints, reviewing various resources rather than depending on an outdated, one-sided standard textbook. Every spring, students requested we write a sea of college recommendation letters. For the eleven consecutive years that worked as a team, we earned placement on the list of faculty favorites.

Personally, our politics clashed, and I lost many an argument because of displaying too much emotion as he battled using logic. Even students realized the differences between us as sometimes we argued in front of them, but they mastered the importance of listening and learned it is acceptable to disagree and still respect one another. At times frustrated, I wanted to wring his neck, but I loved him despite his ultra-conservative beliefs. He was an expert teacher and offered a very different perspective.

After adapting to older kids again, my expertise with at-risk youngsters became obvious to administrators. Year two, my schedule changed.

"We are adding another team-taught partnership to one of your sophomore classes. We think your new partner, Bonnie Lieberman, is a good fit for next year," my chairman informed me.

Bonnie Lieberman, from the Special Education department, a veteran teacher with inner-city classroom experience and special education expertise, became my second partner. We served as surrogate mothers for youngsters needing nurturing, as well as English, reading, and writing instruction. Together, we tried to instill achievable goals in students who often experienced frustration and failure in school. We bounced ideas off each other and our enthusiasm was infectious. With texts containing material that attracted teens and lower literacy that I researched and purchased specifically for the course, we improved students' skill base and accountability. Bonnie was a dynamo who could finish my sentences, run with the stories, and differentiate programs so all students' individual accommodation plans were met. Whether our class earned a bagel breakfast, a donut break, or a simple group hug, we provided what was needed.

I learned that Bonnie's expertise also included EMT certification that allowed me to depend upon her during crises beyond my control.

When a student suffered a seizure, Bonnie yelled, "Let's move, people! Andee, take them outside!"

I froze, unprepared to respond, whereas she belted orders as she protected the victim and assured class safety until the boy was under a nurse's care.

"We need a wheelchair now!" she ordered over the loudspeaker during a second incident.

Bonnie directed me to usher students out of the room when a class member in desperate need of a double lung transplant turned noticeably blue. In a flash, the girl was under nurse's care as Bonnie saved the day again and again.

We were quite a dynamic duo that lasted until my high school days ended about twelve years later. We coped and comforted one another unconditionally through many personal struggles. As I lost both parents, Bonnie battled cancer, had surgery and hip replacements, our spouses lost positions and the school atmosphere became more challenging. Despite the new curricula that focused on test results rather than students' total development, we the two "Brooklynites" felt that we made a difference. Our students loved being in English class.

The administration witnessed my ability to change hats and adapt and I began a third partnership or perhaps, there was a synergistic effect in each of the teams. My schedule now consisted of five junior classes, all team-taught. I remember when the department chair approached Doug Goodrich with the idea of teaming in a second American Studies class; he smiled and addressed me directly, "Fasten your seatbelt and get ready for the ride!"

He worked quickly and efficiently, talked fast and enthusiastically, joked with the students, but at the same time, kept standards high. Students sat awed by his personal history when he shared stories of poverty, dropping out of school and how the Navy saved his life. Since he served in the military, a time etched in his brain, he shared the physical and mental baggage he carried before, during and after the Vietnam War to parallel our reading of Tim O'Brien's *The Things They Carried*, a unique memoir that mixed truth and fiction. Doug displayed the items he carried home, and his descriptive narrative left both the class and me spellbound. Others on our staff chimed in as the Vietnam veterans brought reality to the novel emphasizing that war was not fun and games. Their personal remembrances filled the room with an uneasiness as they relived days etched in their memories that most wanted to forget but never could.

This related to many students in our room from all over the world whose families were victims of war and chaos. They suffered under the Khmer Rouge, fled from religious persecution in Albania and Bosnia-Herzegovina, and talked about bombings in various Middle Eastern countries. Others survived famine in African and poverty in Central American countries, fleeing for better opportunities in America. Panels of students disclosed their pasts, shared their experiences, and brought history alive in our classroom. Silence and tears filled the room as they relived anguish and personal stories.

My five-year partnership with Doug only ended when administration decided to drop American Studies. Counselors then advised and directed students to enroll in traditional English and history courses to increase rigor through drill rather than creative learning for better skill mastery. While the number of students wanting to take our course increased, the number of sections decreased. Classes became less integrated and more traditional. The intention, teaching to the test, was to increase scores and performance on state exams. Although our course integrated multiple intelligences and differentiation focusing on learning styles, administrators followed new guidelines that no longer supported the American Studies layout. Our students had too much fun learning creatively, which often disguised the course rigor and impact.

It was a great run though, and with my partners, we chaperoned students on three-day tours to Boston and Newport, exposing them to historic landmarks, museums, interactive theater, mansions, baseball rivalries and unique cuisine. Unfortunately, at times, financial concerns affected too many students from the lower-socioeconomic group who could not raise the funds to participate, and the trips were eliminated from the curriculum.

Doug regretfully left DHS when our district office offered retirement packages that were too good for some Baby Boomers to refuse. I immediately missed his energy and humor.

Chapter 23

DANBURY HIGH STUDENTS' lives filled my classroom for fourteen years. There were so many special people, but I share a few stories of those who triumphed over insurmountable obstacles and a few who stumbled along the way. Here is a sampling.

Jomaly

How does a teacher ever forget the sad smile and lack of energy that hint of illness? One October morning, Jomaly, a usually engaged, enthusiastic student appeared exhausted, draping the upper half of her body atop the desk.

"What's going on today? Not enough sleep? This is not like you," I remarked.

"Miss, my neck is killing me, and I am so tired," she whined and lifted her heavy head.

Alarmed by her swollen, extended glands, I was sure she had mumps, so I accompanied her to the nurse's office. After a quick check, she advised Jomaly to seek medical attention at once.

"You need to see a doctor, Jomaly. I am calling Mami." I announced.

"My dad doesn't have great coverage, Miss. I only go when I'm sick."

Minimal medical coverage caused an initial delay for care as she and her Mami treated her ailment with hot tea, honey, and lemon, but her situation did not change. After suffering for days without noticing any improvement, Jomaly's mom accompanied her daughter to Danbury Hospital's emergency room. After an examination, Jomaly was admitted for extensive testing. Her doctors' reactions were serious. This was no case of mumps or strep. They scheduled a lengthy battery of tests, x-rays, and scans to determine the root of the problem.

Unaware of the outcome and knowing Jomaly remained under observation, I waited several days and then insisted on visiting. I convinced my teaching colleague that since the hospital was less than a ten-minute drive, he should accompany me after the school day ended. Without hesitation, we drove together during visiting hours to offer support.

Ironically, still wearing her winning smile, she shared the testing results and diagnosis.

"Acute lymphoblastic leukemia!" she announced. "It's attacking my body! The doctors said I need aggressive treatment." Though stunned, I recall how she joked and commented. "Leave it to me to get something that attacks teenage Dominican girls at a higher incidence than other girls." Then, still smiling, she raised her eyebrows and lifted her hands in the air.

In the blink of an eye, disease threatened to kill a teen and rob her of her future. Jomaly's mother depended on a team of experts whose plan was to attack the cancer with aggressive chemotherapy. In preparation, her glorious locks, black hair that cascaded down her spine, were cut as Jomaly chose a pixie hairstyle.

"I don't want to watch my curls just fall out. That's what the doctor said is one of the side effects of chemo. He said my hair will grow back, so I chopped it."

Readying her for treatment, a staff member surgically inserted one port into her chest above her left breast and a second into her skull so that liquid chemo medication could directly attack the cancer. She confessed that she was the baby in the oncology floor and unfortunately, over the course of her treatment, witnessed the death of others who lost the battle she had just begun to fight. Her innocence vanished, replaced with awareness, seriousness, empathy, and strong faith as she fought for health.

As both a parent and her teacher, I ached for her and her helpless mother now overwhelmed with uncertainty, mounting bills, and new responsibilities. Because her immune system was at risk of attack during her treatment regime, Jomaly required home schooling for her own protection. After about two weeks in the hospital, she returned home where I tutored her two days a week covering English and history, sitting at the kitchen table. Many afternoons, we did not make magic but rather worked through her fatigue or pain, the chemo reactions. Although often too tired to complete assignments, Jomaly and her teachers united in agreement to get her through the year. We adapted curricula as needed, but her body weakened and suffered new aches and pains. Her demeanor vacillated as she fought to keep her strength and beat the odds. Some days she coped; others, she threw in the towel. Trying to help her avoid depression, I suggested that she write; poetry was her thing and words flowed as she shared her story. I allowed original works to substitute for formal essays and administered oral quizzes rather than written ones that caused too much exertion. Some days, we worked the entire two-hour slot, but often, I shortened work time because of her sluggish state and just sat with her.

Months passed as the medicine destroyed cancer cells but fatigued her body. She insisted that she would be fine, but her appearance altered as her face took on a puffiness, the side effect of steroids that accompanied the barrage of medication. Saddled with daily aches and pains, she fought her battle bravely, but the disease kept her homebound. Mami pet her daughter's head, signaling understanding and compassion, and prepared café con leche for me every session. During our journey together, her Mami introduced me to delicious Dominican cuisine prepared with care. It was her way of demonstrating gratitude. Between the chicken and rice, *arroz con pollo*, and specialty dishes like *mofongo*, I became a sated honorary family member and lover of Dominican cuisine.

In late spring, close to the term's end, Jomaly's test results indicated marked improvement. She returned to school while continuing outpatient treatment and triumphing. Participating at our Spring Word Fest, a yearly open mic poetry celebration, Jomaly wowed the audience as she recited an original composition describing her ordeal, and won the hearts of peers and faculty. In addition to her award-winning poetry, she morphed into a community role model, a survivor with a purpose whose story armed others with strength.

A year later, she attended the senior prom with a new crop of short curls covered with sparkling jewels styled in an adorable bob hairdo. No one knew that three days prior, she received an additional dose of chemo that robbed her of energy, almost keeping her homebound. But with the encouragement from friends, she agreed to join her peers to celebrate. Mami, a seamstress at a local bridal shop, brought home a slightly damaged baby blue dress and altered it for her Cinderella. Mami had made dresses throughout her childhood and never let her daughter down. Because of her unique creations and precision with a needle and thread, I nicknamed her, *manos de oro* (hands of gold). At the prom, Jomaly glowed and danced with joy knowing that she completed all academic requirements necessary and lost no credits during her long absences. She completed her senior year and would graduate on time! June 2007, despite her residual aches and pains, she proudly marched alongside her classmates as family witnessed their young hero.

Although she thinks that a loss of brain cells still affects her ability to focus and remember, Jomaly enrolled in Naugatuck Junior College courses, intending to pursue education. But financial concerns and commuting interfered so eventually, she left school and sought a permanent job. Perhaps she would return in the future but the present required employment and recuperation.

With her permission, I share her words later in "The Magic Show" collection. Her prose earned second place poetry honors from the Danbury Cultural Society and shared her battle days.

On September 9, 2009, my phone rang, and I heard her familiar voice and sensed her excitement.

"Miss, It's over! No more cancer!"

Her latest bone marrow test indicated that she was cancer free! Finally, she beat the disease! After their placement two years prior, the implanted ports in her skull and chest were removed by her oncologist, completing the final steps to end treatment.

When the Make a Wish Foundation offered her one granted wish, she chose to throw a party, a fundraiser, and donated the proceeds to help others continue their fight against cancer.

"Pay it forward!" she directed.

With unpaid bills and financial woes, she ignored her own needs and gave to others because she had walked in their shoes. She ran half marathons in honor of family and friends who lost their battles, as well as climbed mountains and enjoyed white water rafting in West Virginia with other survivors. Despite her muscle and back issues, she participated, knowing the significance of her efforts.

Chemo took its toll and while it killed the poisonous cancer, it left residual problems she still battles today. We stay in touch as she fights for and with other survivors and shares her story. Her lovely thick curls are back; her smile and determination never left. Her sweet, petite mother, Carmen, stood by her side believing that God's grace would cure her daughter and use her as an example of how faith triumphs and destroys poison. She was correct.

We break bread together occasionally and sit at my kitchen table reminiscing. She recalled how at our end of junior year, I presented her with a glass apple filled with gold glitter. I awarded the apple to a deserving student who "glowed" or lit up the classroom. Of course, the personal joke was that although not radioactive perhaps the rounds of chemo morphed parts of her insides into neon reminders of her battle. We talk of the future, as well. Initially, as a pharmaceutical tech assistant, she still had dreams. Unfortunately, her job offered minimal opportunity for growth and did not provide medical care probably due to her prior condition. Jomaly, a responsible worker, walked to and from work, only missing days when she was under the weather. She finally secured a position in medical supplies with a company that provided health care for her, but during the pandemic, she returned to the pharmacy where she felt appreciated. Although she still juggling jobs, in her spare time, she sits with patients during chemotherapy sessions and insists that she is a reminder that the ordeal will pass. With warmth, positivity, and perseverance she joins fundraisers, walk-a-thons and a plethora of charity events always giving rather than receiving.

Years later, with a clean bill of health and lessoning residual effects, Jomaly still writes. She planned to marry her love, Pasquale aka Pat, but the infamous COVID-19 pandemic forced her wedding date to be postponed twice. From Spring 2020, to Fall 2020 and again to Fall 2021, changes for safety and health were vital. Finally, during November 2021 Jomaly marched down the aisle proudly escorted by her Papi donning a magnificent, jeweled gown and veil, an original created by Mami, of course. She is married, works in a new position, and still maintains her welcoming smile. At times inclement weather triggers her aches but she goes into fight mode and does not give in. She never forgets empathy towards others and possesses one of the biggest hearts possible.

Jomaly taught me perseverance. Her determination and faith are lessons to never give in to despair and always look at the cup as half fun.

Diano

Year after year, I met students who, despite their individual circumstances, needed to become accountable for their actions and understand consequences. Usually, the short hours spent in a classroom cannot compete with the lures of the neighborhood or the lifestyle patterns that impact choices.

In a team-taught class, Bonnie and I created a unique curriculum and bombarded an at- risk group of learners with high-interest, easier readability texts. I convinced my chairperson to put a line item in the budget for a set of books by Walter Dean Myers, a trilogy that engaged my group and sparked reading interest.

I met strikingly handsome Diano during his junior year, and

although he was only seventeen, he was grown beyond his chronological age. The ladies adored him, marveling at his café con leche-colored skin, thick, wavy curls, cleft chin, and the deepest dimples ever seen. For Diano, socializing in school was easy; attacking academics was a different story. Like many of my students, he attended school while working to help a single mother put food on the table. Although his mother painted beautiful landscapes of her native country, Brazil, which were displayed in local library art shows, her artistic talent could not afford them a comfortable life. So, he supplemented her income by working afternoons at a fast-food restaurant and evenings at a local Italian restaurant whose owner/manager permitted him to bring leftover buffet food home to provide dinner and share with his mother in the late evenings. Because his nights were long, he could barely wake for our 7:20 a.m. school day and usually arrived late and tired. Some days, he slept through the alarm causing additional gaps in learning as he missed the first few classes and fell behind in assignments.

Diano needed a wakeup call!

Unlike his peers, Diano had no time to waste anymore; he had no free time because his individual responsibilities also included fatherhood. At fifteen, he became a dad and at age seventeen, Diano tried to share the duties of raising his two-year old daughter. Parenthood changed his carefree reality. Although no longer partnered with his former girlfriend, Diano did not want to lose touch with the little girl whose smile stole his heart. Saddled with a full plate, he needed direction and focus.

With a mixture of teaching, mothering, mentoring and tough love, I attempted to instill another value system, an ethical code unfamiliar to him. I prohibited his bragging aloud about stealing, not reading, and sexual conquests. Since greater maturity was needed, I suggested that he reprioritize. I reminded him that as a provider and a father who dealt with responsibility for his child and himself, he needed first to first earn a diploma. I insisted on completed homework to reinforce new knowledge, participation and time management and he buy into the program. He read his first book, *Monster*, and anxiously waited for part two of the trilogy of books written by Walter Dean Myers. While others provided excuses for haphazard work, Diano turned in essays completed during his night-shift break.

"Sorry Miss, I had no paper, but I did my work. Look. See. Will you take it anyway?" he apologized as he handed me a placemat with menu choices on one side and a hand-written essay on the other!

I eagerly collected his unusual submission and after school, visiting a local Staples, I laminated the menu. Hung on my bulletin board, it served as a reminder to other complainers who were unable to juggle responsibilities and claimed schoolwork couldn't be completed because of parttime jobs. Diano beamed at his accomplishment, his one essay ever displayed by a teacher.

He finished six books that year, read aloud, added to discussions earning an A for the final quarter on his report card which, at seventeen, he displayed on the home refrigerator door. He stopped stealing and he finally acknowledged that a package left by a neighbor's condominium mailbox was no longer free to open or swipe. As he learned, his self-confidence grew, and he was the family's first to graduate from an American high school.

Unfortunately, Diano was clueless when thinking about his future. He juggled jobs, women, and an occasional soccer match with buddies. He had no vision and sought assistance right before the term ended. Abruptly walking out of his senior meeting with his guidance counselor, he admitted feeling lost and disappointed about what goals or opportunities he could pursue.

"Miss, he told me to do some garden work! I wanted to curse that old man out!"

When the counselor suggested "landscaping or garden work", Diano was offended since the profession stereotyped Brazilian and Latinx populations who, without English, tended the local gardens of those wealthier residents in town. I agreed with him that the suggestion was inappropriate and narrow-minded, but I did not have a good response for him.

Discouraged, Diano left the community that summer after

graduation and traveled to Ohio to reinvent himself. He wrote once, spoke of his intention to enroll in a community college but we lost touch. Hopefully, he found purpose and gained success after climbing various hurdles as a young man.

Evelin

They say that good things come in small packages. EG, standing less than five feet tall, is a perfect example. She sat in the last seat, third row, in a class consisting of fifty honor students. Unassuming and quiet, Evelin diligently completed assignments and rarely complained. She only objected when group tasks were assigned in a class of this size. Usually, ten groups of four and two groups of five were assigned to address an issue using members' strengths and cooperative learning to reach a solution. The model allowed differentiation as students could use a variety of modalities to complete the work. As expected, some students became burdened and carried more than their share of the workload while others neglected their duties, passed the buck and depended upon their peers. Evelyn always aimed for A grades and often, frustration overwhelmed her as she was usually group leader by choice.

"Basically, I did this project. If I waited for them, I would lose my A," she complained more than once.

Evelin intended on majoring in sciences to later pursue a medical degree. Although her eye was always on the eventual prize, obstacles appeared impossible to avoid. Born in Mexico, she and her parents fled their native land in search of the American Dream, but during her junior year, reality plagued her journey. While classmates applied for drivers' licenses and parttime work in local stores, she cleaned motel rooms with her mother. Evelin had no entrance papers or green card and despite spending too much money on a local lawyer to resolve the issue, no solution was apparent. Mom and Dad worked and paid taxes while Evelin attended public school knowing that dreams of college were just dreams without possessing the proper credentials.

During dinner preparation as she chopped salad greens, she cried.

"I'm undocumented. I'm chopping away my dreams," she sobbed hopelessly.

We researched solutions, prayed, and waited for a door to open… and it did! When I read of Obama's Dream Act, I knew EG's efforts were not in vain. I called the family.

"Get on the computer. Write in Dream Act," I insisted.

Reading the news changed her life instantly and erased her angst. After immeasurable excitement, Evelin commenced filling out college applications, hoping to focus on the sciences. Her personal statement and her recommendations accompanied a flawless record of her grades. Before long, responses welcomed her as she received and reviewed numerous partial scholarships, assisting her financial need. Eventually, she decided to remain at home and take advantage of a full scholarship to Western Connecticut State University. Knowing she would miss the "dorm life" experience, Evelin remained practical. She could receive her bachelor's degree tuition-free and juggle parttime employment opportunities to help family, as well as save for future higher education costs. Her intention included medical school, so she minimized her spending as she marched on earning A grades in challenging classes.

In the summer of 2015, she applied for a special program to live and study on a university campus. As one of eighty students chosen from 1,000 applicants, she was accepted at both Columbia and Yale. Choosing Yale, she attended a six-week summer internship targeting minorities in pursuit of medical careers. She attended classes, studied endlessly, describing a day that began at 8:00 a.m. and ended after midnight. Smitten with Yale, EG continued schooling with hopes of returning as a medical student, if possible.

Unfortunately, when a very different White House administration did not embrace "dreamers", EG feared living in limbo once again. Putting all her energies into her studies, Evelin completed a summer program at the University of Pennsylvania Perelman School of Medicine focusing on undergraduate research. There, she designed and conducted a pilot mixed-methods study to identify barriers and facilitate enrollment of minority groups in clinical gastrointestinal cancer clinical trials. She worked to recruit underrepresented groups for the trials at Penn Abramson Cancer Center. She then graduated in 2017 with her B.A., majoring in human biology and health studies, ready to move forward.

Next, Evelin gained a position at Harvard University in the Chan School of Public Health. As an interim research project manager, she directed her energy into early childhood obesity prevention for two years. Eventually, she entered their master's program, was named Presidential Scholar, which granted her full tuition and a living stipend. By May 2022, she earned her M.S. in global health & population, infection disease epidemiology. Her résumé continues to expand, and she continues the fight for dreamer equality. Although she is a success story, the instability facing dreamers constantly weighs heavy on her heart.

As a board member of Connecticut Students for a Dream (C4D), she serves as a fiduciary and assists in steering the organization to advance its mission with adequate resources. EG is a community organizer working and lobbying as she assisted in the negotiations to pass SB.4: An Act Assisting Students Without Legal Immigration Status with the cost of college and directs students towards accessing financial aid at state colleges and universities. More recently, she helped host a panel for Latinx students during Hispanic Heritage Month held at her alma mater.

With endless energy packed in this small package, Evelin makes a difference for others unaware of available help. I learned that heroes come in all sizes and inner determination can conquer unforeseen obstacles. She is proof that despite the sneers and negative feedback because of her Mexican heritage or citizenship dilemma, Evelin showed endurance and now is a role model to be reckoned with. I call her another Nunn hero.

The Four Musketeers (Plus Two)

In one American Studies class, four young men destined for success made my day. According to the alphabetical seating chart, the proximity of their desks was ironic since their last names ranged from R to T, keeping them either in one row or adjacent rows where they could kid with one another regularly. They represented the school's diversity. Leighton, a liberal African American; Luis, a liberal Dominican; David, a politically conservative Nicaraguan; and Billy, a liberal Caucasian. Quick-witted, they belittled, as well as praised and supported, one another. Their talents were obvious; they were orators and communicators who could debate, engage, and charm all they encountered. Strong family role models passed batons to these wonderful men destined for success. I cannot fail to include two other cogs on the wheel that were not members of my class but integral parts of this dynamic musketeer group, Ryan, a liberal African American, and Emmanuel, a Nigerian immigrant. All six attended Danbury schools, earned college degrees and are thriving in their various endeavors.

Leighton

Small in stature, but armed with a powerful presence, Leighton embraced education and added spunk and humor to the classroom. Aware of his magnetic personality, I encouraged him, with the assistance of his mother's backing, to enter a speaking contest held at our capital, Hartford. Recognizing his underlying talent, I believed he could represent Danbury favorably and possibly wow an audience. Sponsored by an African American fraternity, the topic was: Black history and the Influence of MLK.

Despite his initial protests, his persistent mother and nagging teacher coaxed him into writing his speech and then practicing its delivery with me. The contest offered a generous incentive that could help with future college finances and the experience could fine-tune his oral communication skills. In February, my young man packed his car and traveled to Hartford with his mother, sister and three cronies for support. Although I was invited to attend, I decided to let him soar on his own. He called with his results later in the evening while I sat in a restaurant in New York City.

"Mama Nunn, we won!"

Leighton earned a $2,500 scholarship for his dynamic oration, and the award would double its value after completing one year of college. After cheering for him and congratulating his success, the carload of joyous companions celebrated as they headed back to Danbury.

One of the most memorable stories about Leighton occurred when he fussed about being assigned to read *The Great Gatsby*, a novel filled with challenging vocabulary and lengthy descriptive passages.

"Mama, I will never get through this! It's dated."

Refusing to agree, I led him through the first three chapters. "Trust me with this. Three chapters, then we will reevaluate."

He groaned but agreed. He became captivated by the timeless story of greed, lies, love and fame and arrived in class one Monday, announcing, "Mama, I finished the book! Wow, never expected that ending!"

He boasted about completing the second half of the story before deadline. I smile as I recall the passionate discussions and creative presentation that assured me of his understanding. His enthusiasm also sparked others to explore the literature and argue over its characters. While delving deeper in the "conspicuous consumption" of the 20s era, the class divided into groups of four or five and played Monopoly. Leighton transformed into one of the robber barons of the time and played with a hunger and thirst for power. It was a different side as he connived to win and steal from opponents. He learned quickly about the opulence of the Roaring 20s and the disastrous crash that closed the era.

On the other hand, when my partner distributed history packets to be completed, Leighton called me to his desk, rejecting the assignment.

"This is busy work and a waste of my time. No way," he flatly refused.

I cajoled and tried to persuade him but standing on principle, he accepted an F for the incomplete packet, lowering his final quarter grade to B.

"No biggie. I've got this Mama." I conceded knowing in my heart that he was right about the unchallenging assignment that filled an hour of class time.

After graduation, Leighton graduated from Hampton College. With degree in hand, he joined Teach for America, who relocated him to Florida to work with academically challenged students a goal he had chosen years prior. He wanted to be the role model for other students of color often complaining that he didn't have many teachers who looked like him. Although he achieved his goal, he called occasionally for advice or to share his frustration. We laughed about the obstacles he faced motivating his audience to keep their eyes on the prize. He thought the job would be a cakewalk, but soon realized that complicated lives were not easily fixed.

"Mama, I got a group of out-of-order kids. How the heck did you always cope? I've got to hand it to you, you never had issues!"

He praised my ability to "control and amuse" and in jest, he suggested that parents give some of them their prescribed meds *before* class so they could be more settled and ready to learn. He persevered, mastered the trade, and eventually left the classroom. He rose to school administrator ready to restructure a hurting system. He married one of his teaching colleagues and is raising a son. Although his mother relocated and sold her home in Danbury, he visits during his rare trips to Danbury or updates me in an occasional text.

Luis

Luis, although raised among three sisters who spoiled him regularly since he was the prince in a household of princesses, was forced to learn patience as the brunt of much cajoling from his buddies. This 6'3" high school football player was blamed regularly by his cronies whenever they were chastised for behavior or just talking too much.

"It was Luis!" one shouted and then they chuckled together as a teacher lambasted him even when it was not his fault. He complained as they threw him under the bus for anything and everything they did.

"It wasn't me!" He pointed to the real culprit, but no one believed him because his smirk was taken for guilt. These were his buddies, so he took their needling and usually let it roll off his back even when my partner changed his seat to control his so-called "poor behavior".

Another A student, Luis earned scholarships and acceptance to University of Connecticut's main Storrs campus where he united with two of the long-time friends to study, party and enjoy college life. After graduation, for a few years, he worked locally using his business degree to move up a corporate ladder. Eventually, he traveled to Atlanta where some family members relocated. They convinced him that the area offered new work opportunities and a good quality of life. He sought a new position in the business field working in computer programming and left his hometown.

Today, Luis is married and raising a daughter. I took a video tour of his lovely home, yard, and basketball court where he welcomes neighborhood kids for a game of hoops. On Christmas in 2022, he drove north to visit family and did not forget about me. With his wife, Maria, and beautiful daughter, he arrived and shared an afternoon reminiscing. His partner is a civil rights lawyer working in Atlanta for KIND (Kids in Need of Defense), an organization devoted to the protection of unaccompanied and separated children.

David

David, the Nicaraguan member of this crew, spent much of his junior year arguing with his peers and me over our political views. At the time, he believed his conservative arguments were sound even though we reminded him how difficult the plight of immigrants was under Republican leadership. We offered him endless documentation but that entire year, he stood steadfast in his beliefs. Eventually, through his short political life his support waned and then under the Trump administration, he witnessed an elite power group gain control and ignore the needs of too many as they stereotyped any Hispanic immigrant and minimized humanitarian causes. Building walls and separating and incarcerating families finally soured his support as he witnessed the biases around him.

After majoring in political science and graduating from the University of Connecticut, he tested many waters. Eventually, CW Post University offered him an admissions counselor position. He works to even the playing field and assure diverse opportunities are available for students of color. At Samba-Safe, he tends to needs for a leading provider of cloud-based mobility risk management software and juggles these positions as he simultaneously raises his son with his long-time partner. David lives locally and I run into him shopping as we're both supporting neighborhood businesses.

Billy

Standing 6'6", Billy's size appeared intimidating on the football field, but in class his body simply blocked the vision of anyone that sat behind him. His peers soon realized he was just an oversized teddy bear. With a witty sense of humor and an ability to intermingle, he fit in perfectly. The crew toyed with him and before long, he was an integral part of their daily bantering.

At twelve, he learned the importance of family unity when his father passed suddenly, leaving his mother to raise Billy and his sister. Life changed, and concerns over finances moved to the forefront. Billy knew he needed good grades and a solid resumé to land where he wanted, Temple University. He attained his goal, but transferred to our local university when financial burdens became overwhelming. He graduated from Western with a communications degree and entered politics. He is presently a legislative liaison for the CT Department of Labor. In addition, he assists with campaigns for those who possess similar ideals. (I can boast that some of the local representatives were past students.) Despite the tough political climate and opposition, he remains dedicated to improving a society that meets the needs of all its members.

Billy married a teacher who shares his ideals, and they are proud parents of two children who stole both hearts.

Ryan

Unassuming, Ryan sat before me in my study hall when I first realized he was another member of the infamous crew. Mild-mannered and soft-spoken, he morphed into a warrior on the football field alongside the musketeers. Raised in a two-parent household, along with an older sister, he learned the value of education and its importance for him to find success. As an African American male, he also knew the obstacles he faced as he was reminded that he had to perform better than white peers to earn positions not often offered to men of color.

He loved math and disliked English, once professing that he had never read a book cover to cover. He bought CliffsNotes and got by without much effort, or so he thought. But as a junior, his English teacher, my friend and colleague, was too savvy for his "getting by" methods and he was forced to work harder than usual. He read the books, he confessed. With a winning smile, he won admirers and when a football injury required pinning together his ankle, he showed no remorse, hopped around, and attended his prom on crutches. He silently triumphed over adversity.

As a scholarship recipient, Ryan also attended college at the University of Connecticut earning a math degree and certification to teach. With experience in various programs helping young people in our community, he was hired by Bridgeport schools to teach mathematics in a diverse setting. He is an educator, as well as a role model for students of color to witness success.

Ryan also gives back to our Danbury community of learners. He offers his own Milton Brown Scholarship honoring his late father whose direction pointed Ryan down the right path. Yearly, he presents this award at a local award ceremony for the Hord Foundation, an organization providing financial assistance to outstanding students of color whose high school performances earn acknowledgement.

Ryan stands as a pillar of our community, reminding others like him that education is a key to many doors of opportunity. Presently raising a wonderful little girl with his partner, he remains a part of my life as I watch him soar.

Emmanuel

Born in Benin, Nigeria, Emmanuel's family migrated to our Danbury community bringing an incomparable work ethic. With a voracious appetite for learning, he set high academic goals understanding that his family expected nothing less from him or his siblings. While his grades were evidence of his commitment, he simultaneously involved himself in student government, sports, and community service activities. Eventually, his profile earned him scholarships and he attended and graduated from the University of Connecticut where he majored in sports management.

Returning to Danbury, he worked in many different businesses including ESPN. More significant, however, is his commitment to humanity. Whether he is digging wells to supply water and building schools to educated youngsters in impoverished towns in Senegal or working with Team-Up, an organization that constructs basketball courts to foster both health and community in Guinee, Emmanuel's efforts are endless.

In Danbury, he honored a deceased friend by building a basketball court in his name at St. Gregory School. If there is a project to foster education or better peoples' living conditions, he is present constructing school buildings, working for Habitat for Humanity or simply lending a hand for anyone in need.

A few years ago, three crew members took me to dinner at a Red Robin in our local mall. I learned then that Luis and Ryan acted out during middle school years, finding themselves in detention often. They admitted that high school changed their behaviors, but they laughed about antics from middle school.

"Not me! My father wasn't having any of that. Nigerian parents don't play. I heard about the sacrifices they made for my brothers and sisters, so I wouldn't dare have school administrator call the house to complain about me. None of us did. And they demanded A grades, so I got A's."

Emmanuel's family left their homeland and expected children to take advantage of all America offered. Today, all the siblings are college graduates. One older brother is an accountant, one in financial services, one sister is a medical doctor, and the baby sister just earned her bachelor's degree.

Fifteen years after they sat in Danbury High classrooms, they keep in touch. We have broken bread together, laughed at my kitchen table, attended awards ceremonies, funerals, celebrations and offered advice when summoned. With the births of their newly created generation, they pass on lessons of inner strength, empathy, patience, and respect. Imbedded in my memories, I am thankful for the honor of knowing the six Musketeers.

Myeisha

Every once in a while, I am reminded that years pass too swiftly. Prior students become adults and/or parents pretty quickly. More than once on opening day, an enthusiastic student announced that I taught their parent. This immediately aged me since more than twenty years had flown by! In 1989, for example, sophomore, Tanya Perkins, sat in my Henry Abbott Technical HS reading class when I reentered the education field after a ten-year hiatus to raise my babies. Tanya was a lovely, tiny bit of a thing who donned the widest smile and was liked by all. Her long-term goal was to enter the nursing profession, but starting motherhood detoured her plans.

Fast-forward about twenty years. Myeisha enrolled in my DHS American Studies class and raised her hand. "Ms. Nunn, do you remember Tanya Perkins? She had you at Tech."

Before I could respond, she added, "That's my mom!"

Father time was paying me a visit! This reality check proved that years marched on. I could change my hair color, update my style, continue to perfect my craft, but I could not stop the aging process. I Had matured but could still impact those who sat in my classroom. The bubbly sixteen-year-old daughter fared well in high school, became avidly involved in the current-events portion of our curriculum, loved politics and public policy. After many years, her mother returned to her studies to earn a nursing degree, while juggling jobs, monitoring her children, and supporting their endeavors.

In 2015, while enrolled in the University of Hartford, Myeisha earned an intern position in The White House assisting with public events. During one special yearly event, Myeisha spotted a familiar face in the crowd of invited visitors. Recalling the photos tacked on my classroom bulletin board, she recognized a face.

"Excuse me, but are you Mrs. Nunn's daughter?"

Ilana nodded.

"I'm Myeisha and I was in your mom's class. She always talked about you and your sister."

Ilana introduced her husband and my granddaughter. They participated in the yearly easter egg hunt celebrated with President Obama and First Lady Michelle.

"Could I take a picture with you and your family?" She was too excited.

A bystander snaped a photo and Myeisha emailed it to my Western address. She also informed me that after many roadblocks, her mom was completing her degree, fulfilling a lifelong dream, and planning to graduate as a registered nurse.

Myeisha graduated from University of Hartford's Honor program. She took advantage of travel/study programs and spent time in Hawaii, Ireland and DC forever broadening her horizons. Afterwards, she relocated, moved to Silver Springs, Maryland, and accepted a fellowship position from a nonprofit organization focused on improving voting procedures. After majoring in politics, she understood that DC could offer her more opportunities than Danbury. She credited her introduction to current events in my course with partner, Joe Vas, as the spark that refocused her career.

Before her July departure, she contacted me desiring to reunite for an afternoon of talk and eats. Both Myeisha and her mom, Tanya, joined me in my home for a luncheon date filled with good memories and exciting discussions about future endeavors.

On October 18, 2018, the dynamic pair were my guests at the yearly NAACP Awards dinner themed, "Defeat Hate: Vote". The organization's chairperson chose Myeisha to introduce me as one of the year's recipients of the Excellence in Education Award. Gleaming, I boasted over the accomplishments of five students who joined me. What a proud night!

In 2021, amid the COVID-19 epidemic, Myeisha graduated from NYU's master's program in public policy. By 2023, she was working as a senior analyst in management and strategy with Goldman Sachs. Her mother was employed as the RN she had always wanted to be.

Luis

Although the dating game gets tricky when religion and ethnicity become variables to consider, I am not the only success story I know. Some dare to step outside their comfort zone or family expectations to change the perception of what can or cannot be possible. Recently, I rewatched the movie, "Loving", the true story of interracial love and forbidden marriage. In Virginia as late as 1970, miscegenation was illegal and couples that broke the law faced long prison sentences. The vitriol I witnessed in the film reinforced that a lack of tolerance and sensitivity towards others different from ourselves is alive and well. I am not sure what makes others pass judgment about subjects that are foreign to them.

This subject reminds me of a young Puerto Rican student who sat in a middle row, last seat in my advanced American Studies class. Reserved and observant, he absorbed everything offered. He rarely added to group discussions, but when he did speak, his brilliance shone. Both sides of his brain hinted intelligence: he wrote poetry and well-developed, supported essays while enrolled in AP Science and Math courses preparing him for a medical career. He was far from anti-social, but he chose friendships carefully as he focused on academic achievement and dismissed the typical teenage drama surrounding him. In his dream, he was headed to UConn on an academic and financial need-based scholarship.

Then the unexpected: he fell in "teenage love" with the wrong girl. She didn't speak Spanish, know his culture, or even look like a candidate he could bring home to Mother.

The young lady, also an honor student, believed her Cambodian family would never embrace Luis. Her parents pushed education and expected their daughters to attend UConn on scholarships. After all, the sacrifices of suffering under the Khmer Rouge and finally leaving a war- torn country to seek the American Dream was a constant reminder of children's responsibilities. Offspring frequently felt guilt and family futures depended upon their success. Education was key and hopes became a reality in April when an acceptance letter invited Kim to enroll in the University of CT at minimal cost. So far, her parents' dreams were coming true. The good daughter's academic work ethic was rewarded, and with discretion, she simultaneously followed her heart.

The clandestine couple shared the school days during their senior year and maintained a relationship rarely enjoying time together outside the school setting. Ironically, dreams of UConn came true for both, but the hidden relationship gnawed at their hearts. What about senior prom? Would they escort other friends and meet at the event? Would their secret friendship ever be permitted? They mapped out many possible plans and then unexpectedly, senior award night happened to change the situation as both sets of parents sat nowhere near one another to witness their children's successes.

In the auditorium, Luis's name echoed from the stage as he received multiple rewards for his academic accomplishments. Proud family members shouted gleefully when they realized that Luis's efforts were acknowledged with financial gifts to pay his total college costs. Kim also was honored that night and beamed more often over her secret boyfriend's accolades than her own. As the program came to an end, understanding how her father valued academic prowess, she dared introduce Luis as her "good friend, a school buddy." Dad nodded in approval at the talented young man, noting his many trips to the podium.

"Smart boy! You received much attention tonight." He smiled. He admired intelligence and acknowledged that Luis must be intelligent.

Days after the initial encounter, Mr. T, Kim's father, surprisingly agreed with Kim's suggestion that her friend, Luis, might escort her to the senior prom. Publicly, the two could attend the festivities without fear. This could be a nice ending, but there is a nicer one. The two attended UConn and maintained their relationship eventually with families' approval. Both graduated with degrees in bio-molecular sciences and pursued careers in research. Married, they celebrate their diversity and strong familial ties. Today, the couple is raising a daughter.

Chapter 24

MOVING TO DANBURY offered my family a rich celebration of cultural diversity that instilled sensitivity and embraced difference. Students from fifty different backgrounds speaking forty different languages filled the classroom seats, and their stories were rich with unique traditions. Some families simply relocated to America for educational opportunities while others fled war-torn countries and sought safety. From Eastern European countries like Bosnia and Albania, African nations like Nigeria and Ghana, Middle Eastern nations like Lebanon, Central and South American places like Ecuador, Dominican Republic, and Brazil and finally, Southeast Asian countries like Vietnam, Laos, and Cambodia; the list is endless. They shared their cultural differences with one thing in common: all sought the American Dream of happiness and success. Where better than in an American Studies classroom could I learn so much from so many.

When I began teaching the course, colleagues related the quest of the "boat people" Southeast Asian families who sought refuge after the Khmer Rouge overpowered their lands torturing or slaughtering the opposition. The parents of my students witnessed murders, rapes, burning villages and fled their homelands as conditions worsened and Communism overpowered their countries taking away lives as they once cherished. Leaving all they owned, they arrived and planted roots in, of all places, Danbury, Connecticut. Their children were their new hope and all they sacrificed was for survival. Many worked two or three jobs trying to make ends meet as they locked their scars away and robotically charged ahead. In the new environment, children were their hope, their future and with high expectations, they demanded perfection from their fruits. They were given American names so that their assimilation into the school system would appear easier as they learned English and studied, but at home, their traditions separated them from other classmates. Fear of losing identity led parents to forbid crossing cultures, but rather, instilled staying with one's own kind.

There are so many successes despite the pressures, but this lengthy introduction brings one tragedy to the forefront. I will call her Cookie, the bright, sweet young Cambodian lady who as a junior, aspired to attend UConn on a scholarship. Her grades warranted recognition and she filled her resumé with extracurricular activities and admirable community service. Because of her reserved personality and quiet demeanor, the American Studies class forced her to step out of her comfort zone since requirements included presentations and group work, as well as individual projects. She forced herself to increase her volume, address an audience with eye contact and practice presentation skills to earn her A grade in both history and English components of the course. This met her parents' expectations, so without pats on the back, she continued pursuing academic success in other classes as well.

Secretly, she bonded with a young African American male knowing that disapproving parents would never find the relationship even a remote possibility. First, dating of any kind was discouraged—it interfered with school learning. Second, any relationship that crossed racial lines was forbidden. As such, Cookie knew she was overstepping and had to be cautious as she hid her involvement from parents.

She hid the extent of her intimacy from everyone including most of her friends. Without prenatal care, she also hid her pregnancy. No one noticed the weight gain or the wardrobe changes that covered her secret. Believing she would be disowned, she silently carried her unborn child and the dilemma of what to do. The boy was in his own denial and separated himself from the problem, believing he might not have fathered this child and thus, it became Cookie's solo journey.

I cannot imagine her fear, loneliness and panic the morning she went into labor at home. Alone and locked in a bathroom, she delivered a child. Logically, one knows that help is necessary and should immediately be at hand. That did not happen. Shame filled the room and Cookie believed she would be banished by her father. Logic left. No thoughts of taking the baby to the firehouse or the police station or a church. Logic and sanity disappeared as she took life from the newborn.

Details became public during her trial. The incident was discovered when Cookie's mother took her to the hospital because of extensive bleeding. After examination, doctors determined a recent birth and then an investigation about a baby's whereabouts began. Police reports indicated that Cookie's mother attempted to cover up the dastardly deed and discarded the infant to save her daughter from a father's wrath. A distraught, lost seventeen-year-old girl was sentenced to eighteen years in prison. I cannot fathom how anguished she must have felt alone on that cold floor. A harsh sentence, although punishment was deserved.

Sadness permeated our town that day.

About nine years later, the case was reviewed, and Cookie was released from prison. She returned to a newly supportive family that opened their doors and embraced their child. She pursued her education. Rumor has it that she finished college at Southern and may consider law school. She juggles parenting and working as is an entrepreneur who opened her own business, with eyes on the future.

Chapter 25

PART OF THE American experience included a three-day/two-night-stay adventure aimed at New England, specifically Boston and Newport. Yearly, we revised our itinerary to spark interest and enrollment. Three to four filled buses ventured north to visit places like: JFK Museum, Mark Twain's home, Faneuil Hall, the Freedom Trail, as well as tours of Newport's mansions including The Breakers. We attended an interactive mystery play providing a theater experience, toured naval vessels, walked through museums and local cemeteries, and ate in a variety of restaurants.

Teachers longed for seafood specialties or Italian food in Boston's North End while students favored hot wings, Dale and Thomas' unique popcorn and fast food more affordable selections. We slept in motels that included breakfast buffets and assigned four students to a room to help stretch limited budgets. Some of our student body members paid the $240 cost in one payment while others struggled and budgeted payments over five months so parent paychecks or their own parttime earnings could meet the financial requirements. A few special cases were awarded scholarships for a one-time school opportunity. For the most part, all went well. Yet, eight years of trips did have some memorable highlights:

- **Yankee vs Red Sox game:** One of our boisterous Yankee fans elected to rip an opposing team Boston T-shirt in half much to the dismay of a local, drunken fan. The Bostonian promised to retaliate.

  "I'm going to kick your ass kid!" he shouted angrily.

  Aware of his threat, we left the arena and swiftly walked towards our bus back to the motel. But when we reached the corner, I noticed the inebriated man was mulling around checking out which bus our silly fan would board. The attacker boldly snatched our boy's Yankee hat as he approached the bus folding door and the frozen victim stood before him in shock.

  "Let him learn a lesson. It could teach him to shut his big mouth," remarked the assistant principal who accompanied us.

  I ignored her, knowing the adults were responsible for student safety and instinctively pushed ahead placing myself at the bus entrance standing between the student and the attacker.

  "I got this," I stated emphatically, smiled, and snatched the hat back as I scooted our smart aleck boy onto the bus with a few hat swats. My Bed-Sty experience supplied my "know how" and I quelled the incident, which caused the permanent elimination of a professional baseball game from the next year's "to do" list. Yet, I stood out as a legend as I talked the aggressor down and swiftly led the student to safety. Rumors spread about how the large overly tattooed, drunken enemy was taken down by little Ms. Nunn. The story was exaggerated more and more over time, but I enjoyed the accolades.

- **Shaved ice in the eye:** Too much frolicking in motel hallways caused an unfortunate event. After jostling for position at the ice machine, a male student playfully threw ice chips as he flirted with a classmate. The game ceased when one handful of ice hit the girl's eye, more specifically her cornea. Accidents and carelessness happen but fearing a tear, one colleague volunteered to forfeit the rest of the trip time to accompany the lone victim by bus back to Danbury for medical care. The aggressor apologized, fearing repercussions, but his guilt was enough punishment at the time. Unfortunately, losing one bus forced fifty students to squeeze three bodies into a seat designed for two. It made for an uncomfortably long journey home the following day. Fortunately, the injured student did not suffer any permanent damage.

- **Newport police intervention**: One of our girls decided to shoplift a CD record from a local store rather than spend her limited funds until when exiting the store, alarms rang, and the police arrived.

  "Wasn't me," she denied but we knew she was the culprit.

  Although she attempted to drop the item before leaving and claim innocence, her guilt was obvious. As a group, we stood out already as tourists who did not resemble the inhabitants of this wealthy, quaint environment and now, negative attention could reinforce racial stereotypes and mar the entire group of innocent students. Although we wanted to kill this kid, somehow, we reiterated our concern, coaxed the officer, and begged that we be permitted to punish the culprit on our territory. We were pleasantly surprised when he caved in. We whisked her into the bus as the assistant principal yelled, threatened, and probably took a few years off her life.

- **Ralph Lauren's car exhibit**: After boring the bunch in a museum where hawks described as "security guards" watched our every move, waiting for us to spoil an exhibit, we needed to excite the group. Enough of the DO NOT TOUCH exhibits. Change was imperative. One of my partners discovered a Lauren car exhibit, bribed a guard, and rerouted the entire group to a room that housed ten luxury rides from the twenties to the present-day Ferraris. Some noted that one oversized convertible sedan with its deep army green exterior and luxurious camel leather interior resemblance to a Gatsby car we read about in class.

"Miss Nunn, conspicuous consumption, right," he smiled, and I approved his correct connection to text.

The boys marveled and voted it the favorite activity of the week. Their cameras flashed, and some even called fathers and brothers sharing their excitement.

- **Eating**: A hot wings contest almost destroyed student, David Z! Demonstrating his invincibility towards "hot" spices, he attempted to break a record by woofing down wings followed by milk chasers to cool the fire raging in his esophagus. As his face changed colors, he persevered, but I was glad this took place on the final day of the adventure since about an hour later, he appeared ill.

- **Elevator duty**: I sat adjacent to the elevator doors in pajama pants and T-shirt as I monitored the motel rooms, making certain there was no "hanky-panky" among my sixteen-year-old students. We taped doorknobs, warning that cut tape meant leaving the room without permission and facing con-sequences, but that did not stop some raging hormonal males from finding excuses to wander halls searching for any kind of action ranging from gambling card games to love connections. Claiming the need for ice or a soft drink, boys wandered out unaware that I was posted as warden since our paid security guard wandered all floors and could miss the sneakiest of students who timed his walk.

"Oops, sorry Miss."

More than once, heads peered out, took one glance at my stoic face and U-turned into their rooms. After all, I am a mother whose daughters had attended field trips and already knew what could or would happen without monitoring teenagers!

- **Roommate:** I shared a room with a wonderfully creative English teacher. Although quick-witted and entertaining, she neglected to reveal one important fact that impacted my nights' sleep. She suffered from a breathing/sleep disorder that she remedied by using a breathing machine. Donning a facemask, she resembled Hannibal Lecter, and I knew I needed to sleep facing the wall, but that wasn't enough. Her mask connected to a large, loud machine that pulsated with every breath taken. The noise resembled the sound made by ER equipment with air compressions rising and falling all night. Tempted to pull the plug, I refrained, realizing I could kill my roomie, so I overdosed on Nyquil and held my hands over my ears since no earplugs were available until a few hours of sleep took over. I later learned that the room assigner, someone I considered a dear mentor *before* this incident chose to eliminate the information to maximize our budget using two-person room occupancy.

Chapter 26

IT IS NEVER fair that we teachers observe many sad faces that fill a room. While educators in administrative roles worry about data and high-stakes testing, they forget about the variables that are not easily measured.

The stories are endless and unfortunately, the baggage never seems to disappear. It is not simply the lack of computer access to complete assignments and compete with entitled peers. With economic issues plaguing the country, more students are hungry, tired, living in shelters, homeless or simply without resources to facilitate learning in our modern world. Too many families are not cohesive and battle financial instability that rattle its members. Fears of lockdowns, outsiders, loss of power and safety, gang violence and war are endless. Loss of innocence, loss of childhood, devastates my student population.

So many share tales of sexual abuse in which brothers or uncles or fathers forced ashamed daughters to succumb to their desires. I witnessed attractive girls transform themselves into unfeminine, asexual teens as a means of protection. Others learned to thrive on their sexuality, thinking it was their only worthwhile trait that needed to be flaunted.

Jay reeked with sadness and despair. Her classroom writing intimated sexual behaviors unacceptable for a sophomore fifteen-year-old to experience. I learned that her father had been molesting her as soon as her body showed signs of womanhood. He served jail time for some illegal behavior, but he returned to the home and its reoccurring abuse. DCS (Danbury Child Services) knew the case, Guidance Department knew the case and now, I reopened Pandora's box searching for a child's safety. After all, I was required to act as designated report if any hints of inappropriate behavior or indications of abuse arose. This story shocked me and reinforced my feelings about how the system fails many in need.

It had been reported repeatedly that Jay was not safe, but each time DCS initiated an attempt to remove Jay from her home, at the last moment, she turned down the opportunity, reversed her story and denied the abuse. Why?

"She admits and then backs down. It's sick in that house. Rumor has it that she is the main caretaker for her severely disabled younger brother."

As soon as the school day ended, her homecare worker job began. Jay feared that if she was removed from the home, her brother might die from neglect. Relieved not to deal with her husband's advances, Jay's mother allowed her daughter to be her substitute. She also gave up mothering her handicapped son after 2:00 p.m. when her daughter returned from school. She claimed it was too tiring carrying around and diapering a heavy nine-year-old unable to fend for himself.

Jay became the surrogate wife and mother. Sadly, social services felt Jay tied their hands when she refused their intervention and lied so that she could serve her brother. Chaos continued, and her brother remained the sole recipient of her love and he gave her purpose.

She found respite reading, a pastime that for short breaks took her away from the hellish drama she faced. Reality disappeared and fantasy worlds diminished her pain when she traded her reality for an author's imaginary creation. Whenever possible, her face was stuck in a book.

One Sunday morning, I met her at a church where my family occasionally joined services to worship. Church services began at 11:00 and ran, as the pastor would say, "until we were finished praising", usually close to 1:00 p.m.

Carrying *To Kill a Mockingbird,* Jay shared her church duties. "I monitor the babies in the nursery while parents attend service. When they are all okay, I have time to read a chapter. I'm good with kids and I also have my brother in the room."

Before we parted, she shared additional news. "My dad is playing piano today. Sometimes he accompanies the choir. In fact, this week's offering is being collected to purchase a specially equipped van we desperately need to transport my brother."

She sounded excited about the prospect of purchasing the equipment. I nodded.

She failed to realize that I knew much about the history of her home life. Heavy-hearted, I sat with my daughters in the pews, observing the unaccountable perpetrator sitting on the piano bench atop the dais, and almost lost my breakfast. Seething, I couldn't stay and witness his hypocrisy; I gathered the girls without explanation and left after the first song ended. Eventually, I told my daughters why the swift departure and debated as to whether I should share what I knew with the preacher.

I chose not to intervene knowing that the pastor would always give repentant congregants a new chance. Surely, he must have known about the jailtime and the man's proclivity but perhaps he thought it was under control. Since social services dropped the case, so did I. Guilt plagued my mind every time Jay quietly took her seat in sophomore English class.

Unless her brother was ill, she attended school regularly and often bearing unexpected jewelry gifts. Once it was a pair of prayer hands, and a second time, an angel pin. At the end of class, without a word, she presented them to me, wearing her usual sad look. I accepted them with a hug, but I knew I could not save her. Although she was my student only one year, I saw her a few times until her graduation. When chaperoning the senior prom, I observed her looking more radiant than usual, but she still did not appear happy. While peers received acceptance letters, she made no college plans, had no future aspirations, and settled for a minimum-wage job to make extra change when she wasn't tending to her brother's needs.

Years later, on a late fall afternoon, I joined a friend for a quick latte. Before entering the eatery, walking towards me, more than ten years after she left my class, I faced Jay. Accompanied by one adult and a child, she first introduced her mother, a poorly groomed woman in her late forties who barely acknowledged the encounter. Next, I met her own six-year-old daughter. There was no ring on Jay's finger, no mention of a special man. Sadness still permeated Jay's eyes and that lost expression remained. We hugged, and then I addressed the child.

"You have a wonderful mommy. She was so smart in my class! She loved to read and gobbled up more books than all the other students. Did you know she also wrote poetry?"

The child shrugged and then answered, "I like when Mommy reads to me."

"That's so special. Keep making her read to you and let her teach you how to read!" I suggested.

"I already know my letters," she boasted.

"Another smartie pants!" I added before saying goodbyes.

Studying their faces, I noticed the overly strong resemblance. The little girl's face mirrored both Jay and her father. I believe the sick cycle that permeates the family continues, but I can't ask.

Sadly, many cries for help go ignored and the system fails until a class writing assignment opens a chest burdened by secrets finally shared. For me, access to the school social workers, psychologist, and health-based centers are more important than finding deans of discipline and testing data. Empowering students and freeing them from burdens that impede their success is vital in healthy development. I learned that it does take a community to help these students.

Unique faces from nations of the world sit together in search of America's promised dream of better lives. Trying to assimilate, they battle language struggles and raise siblings while their parents juggle jobs trying to make ends meet. Some hide the secret of being undocumented for fear of deportation, a common occurrence that tears families apart. All of them move like checker pieces from ESL (English as a second language) to ELL (English language learners) to transitional classes and although they learn the language, they prematurely face tests that negate their abilities and label them failures. They learn literal English, but do not understand the nuances and inferences of higher-order comprehension.

We have yet to close achievement gaps. We have yet to end bias and stereotypes. We have yet to acknowledge that it is a compilation of variables that are accountable for student learning. There is no panacea. Whether educators individualize instruction or differentiate to meet needs or enforce adaptations to attempt to make curriculum meet the needs of all, outside variables profoundly make the playing field uneven.

I kept many pieces they wrote, hoping to share them so others develop the empathy to understand that those taking seats in every class all have unique stories. The way they conduct themselves is a result of their experiences and the scars embedded in their lives.

My message to colleagues and the public-at-large is simple: all students must have access to quality and targeted educational opportunities. To prepare young adults to be our future leaders and productive citizens, we must recognize and address the socioeconomic factors that negatively impact and compromise academic achievement and success. The multicultural composition of our community makes it imperative that teachers become culturally competent; that they listen to the different voices to equalize the arena in which student development is molded. The idea of banning books and "protecting" students from learning factual truth is unacceptable in an arena where knowledge eradicates ignorance rather than promotes guilt. Teachers who understand difference are better able to find solutions that maximize productivity and achievement and minimize failure.

Academic performance and educational standards need to improve concomitantly with teacher expectations. It is important, however, to understand that teachers alone can't be expected to be the panacea for societal problems and changes. Teachers and families must partner in responsibilities to students. Both must foster collaboration and cooperation to bridge the communication gaps that hinder student growth. Elimination of all problems is not possible, but we can change the way we face them. Whatever challenges and barriers confront us must be broken down into manageable pieces. As teachers, we must use these lessons to build solutions.

Teachers are charged with providing a safe, vital, and interesting place for learning in competition to omnipresent video games, iPads, or chat rooms. It is an uphill battle to instill a love for learning, for reading a good book, which can supersede these attractions. Cultural awareness, community support, financial backing, and adequate resources (books, computers etc.) are the building blocks to finding those creative solutions. Yet, first and foremost, teachers need to be passionate about students and subject matter. If they miss one of these components, they cheat their audience and themselves.

Chapter 27

DAILY, AT 1:30 p.m., a train of yellow buses parked and surrounded both the front and back of the school building exits waiting for the 2:00 dismissal bell. They transported most of our students to Danbury neighborhoods located off eight exits on I-84. Their travel routes caused traffic delays around the city typically, making my ten-minute ride home into a thirty-minute commute. Knowing this inconvenience, most of the faculty delayed leaving school to avoid the congestion.

I was famished by the time I arrived home after 2:30 because lunch break at 11:00 usually served as my breakfast. I grabbed a snack and typically shared my day's events with Ronnie whenever his schedule provided days off during the week. Knowing my desire to engage, he glanced up from either watching the news or filing a work report and inquired, "How was your day?"

I proceeded to ramble on about some student's poem, a crisis resolved in class, or a teaching moment that exploded into great discussion. I assumed he listened and filtered what he heard. As a communications major, I was aware of his selective listening, so I threw questions at him to hold him accountable and to assure myself that I was not talking to the air. He gave about 75% correct feedback, not too shabby.

After my reporting, I checked my laptop computer, a gift from my elder daughter who insisted I upgrade to newer technology rather than my antiquated computer. And frankly, she was correct, as I needed to learn some new technology. With practice, I adopted Ronnie's half listening and paying attention while doing other things, so I could check search engines or log onto my email account during our conversations.

A website called Classmates posted "one new message". A bit curious, I checked. It read from March 26: "Hello young lady! How are you?" That was it except for the sender's name, Forrest! Intrigued and excited, my heart pounded. Through eyes welded with tears, I blurted, "Ronnie, I think it's Forrest! Oh my God! How can it be? What do I say?"

"Calm down. Make sure it's him. Too many fakes prowl the Internet."

I needed to be careful since the web, though wondrous, had some shaky characters invading privacy. So, I responded simply, "If it's you, you were very special to me. How do you know me and how old are you now?"

I breathed, pressed "send" and hoped for a timely answer.

The response was not immediate. I waited impatiently. And then, three days later, it arrived: "I am that person, will be 51 in August. You were a very special teacher as well. I remember you from J.H.S. 35, are you that Andee? I'm in Florida, decided to say hello. Wow, I think it is you!"

Shocked by the unexpected contact, I answered him with a brief, polite response because so much time had passed. We hardly knew one another. "Yes, I am that Andee. It is a bit surprising to hear from you. I hope you are happy and well. It's been such a long time."

I needed to tread carefully.

He wrote:

Thanks for your response, I am just as much in shock. I was just on this computer fooling around one day and decided to look up your name, one thing led to another and now here we are. Wow! My life has gone well, I've been married for a lot of years now, I am the father of three young adults, have a home and business owner here in West Central Florida.

Now I am communicating with one of the most important persons to ever been a part of my life. Life is so good right about now! This poor kid from Brooklyn with the long eye lashes (smile) would like to thank you, for your intervention those many years ago. You made the difference in my life. I just don't know how I could ever repay you other than saying that you will always be my teacher of the year! Tell your family I said hello, tell your students about this used to be poor kid from Brooklyn who says that you are a difference maker and pay attention (smile). Thanks, will always think of you!

Once again thank you for your response, it is very nice to know that I have been thought of in a favorable way. I am very happy to hear of all your family's success, from great parents come even greater children congratulations. You know several weeks ago I was channel checking and heard the name Ilana, I saw this very pretty young lady who just so happened to be a publicist from NY, and I started thinking of you, could that have been your daughter? If so wow! I have been married to the most amazing women, for over twenty-five years now. She put the icing on the cake, that you began so many years ago (smile) and I just love her with all my heart! It is very nice to have a person who loves you, for you!

Thanks for the conversations on how to treat a lady, they have served me well…very well (smile). However, when it came time for the naming of my two daughters, it was hands off. [They're] great young ladies but very spoiled. I was able to name my son. My wife and I have owned a trucking business for a few years, although good I'm ready to venture off now, maybe retire or work for someone else, with the price of fuel being so high. I have other prospective irons in the fire…life is good. Tell Mr. Nunn I would have loved to play him a game of basketball back in the day even though I know he was a professional. Tell him I was a professional street baller if there is such a thing (smile). Well Mrs. Nunn I must go now, may Gods' blessings continue to be bestowed upon your family and with his grace, may they continue to prosper! Forrest.

Our writing began back and forth, on and off, sharing bits and pieces about our lives. I wanted to know everything, and he reciprocated. During the first few months, we messaged weekly and then one July morning while I was writing on the computer, the telephone rang. I did not recognize the deep resonant voice, so I cordially asked, "Who is this please?" In our home no one ever disclosed who was speaking before a caller identified their name first. Because of Ronnie's travel schedule, three women were often alone, so it became standard procedure to ask, "Who is this please?" Assuming this was a typical sales pitch or donation request, I parroted, "Who is this please?"

I continued my typing.

"Hello young lady, it's me, Forrest."

For a brief time, our conversations were a dialogue of two cautious people who did not dare tread too quickly into unsettling water, with surface talk. But facades disappeared, and after the initial excitement, Forrest and I erased the awkward silence that had grown over time and interrupted our friendship.

Years melted away as we rekindled our friendship. We talked of good and bad times and important decisions like marriages, parenting and traveling. His life led him to enlist in the army at seventeen and as rumored, lying about his actual age. The experience redirected his life as his assignments sent him to Germany and later to Hawaii. He met his wife in the service, married young and later, when discharged from the army, the couple made a home near Tampa, Florida and started a family. He boasted about his son, two daughters and special grandson, who he chose to raise.

We spoke about our special connection in Brooklyn, how we impacted each other's life and how we both never forgot our bond. Over the summer, our short talks became longer ones, and we began sharing different perceptions of the same series of events, the same story of how two unique lives came together. He remembered events through the eyes of a "man-child", and I remembered them as a naïve, young teacher. We walked, or should I say, talked our way down memory lane comparing our jarring recollections, correcting one another, and filling in the gaps that time created.

I shared our "reunion" with my family and listened curiously to their different reactions.

"Good for you, Mom."

My younger daughter realized how important this relationship was for me. She read excerpts and offered her approval, but later suggested I not forward every bit of writing, but rather, wait until it was a complete story. She applauded how teacher and student communicated so easily after such a long absence. "You certainly have a special bond, Mom. After all those years too! You were about twenty-nine and he was eighteen when you parted. And he finds you thirty years later? OMG."

Her sister's view was quite the opposite. "Be careful, Mom. You never know."

She cautioned me about my exuberance, suggesting that I not be careless about spilling my past onto paper with a stranger. Initially, she dismissed the reconnecting and catching up until she repeatedly heard my passion and reluctantly became more accepting.

My husband thought it was a terrific idea, and my sister transformed into my editor and critic who read everything both Forrest and I shared. When I mentioned what was happening with a few closer colleagues, they applauded the effort, awed by the special connection even though years lapsed, but their interest waned. But I did not need anyone to support my effort; I bought in, Forrest bought in and that was all that mattered to me. I celebrated the memories.

Perhaps, it will be my story, my legacy, passed down to my grandchildren.

I learned that Forrest's commitment to writing me about his life meant opening a Pandora's box for him. Ironically, this successful man who overcame obstacles that for many would have been insurmountable burdens, never shared his secret past with anyone. His wife and children were yet to learn about the burdens and challenges of his youth.

I listened to the truth, the reality of why he had needed me so badly and how lost he felt when I left him in Long Island so many years ago. "You just walked out of my life, period."

Wounded by the separation, I heard how he misinterpreted the event as a desertion and realized why it was important to reunite. He learned that he was a part of me all those years, the subject of so many lessons shared with my classes. "You never left my thoughts and prayers."

Yearly, I used our story to help mold young lives, to emphasize how a teacher learned from a student and how mentoring that student affected his life decisions.

Chapter 28

FORREST AND I kept writing and sharing. For me, his intimate stories reinforced the importance of understanding the students before me. According to Forrest, mentors made a difference, and the key was listening and encouraging. In order to make students more productive, I had to realize their truths, which often included daily responsibilities that interfered with their learning and my teaching. I needed to find alternative strategies to empower them to succeed. I had conversations with Forrest regularly and listened to his suggestions. He often repeated the same thing.

"Kids are kids, different packages but still kids. You KNOW kids. You reached me, Missy. Remember? You got the magic. Maybe I need to talk to some of those knuckleheads for you?"

Grateful for his input, I declined his offer but always used him as an example. Every student heard my Forrest stories. I kept encouraging/fostering their interest in learning, but after decades of teaching, I noticed some significant changes. Kids may still be kids, but times were different.

The world changed. Computer access brought many options. The Internet, along with its benefits, offered the ability for students to encounter unsavory characters on various platforms who preyed upon youth. When not monitored, young people could find inappropriate material at their fingertips, become intrigued, and mimic behaviors too advanced and dangerous for their ages. Amid a media blitz of sex, drugs and violence, temptations to engage in at-risk behaviors intensified. Some teens rushed to grow up but lacked the life skills to handle and realize the consequences of their actions.

Thankfully, Forrest and I rekindled our story and he talked and offered suggestions.

"I'm from the street. I know the mindsets of too many lost kids. Run the stories by me and maybe this kid from Brooklyn can still teach you something, haha."

I shared many issues. He called me his sanctuary, and I called him my transformer. There would be no response to equal the size of devastation one early afternoon in December 2012, however, when uncertainty and fear permeated the building. I was attending a mandatory two-hour workshop with eleventh grade English teachers held in a conference room located in our library. Regular classes were covered as this select group met with a state representative to discuss yearly testing procedures and data collection. With policies changed, the state provided a curriculum specialist to train teachers on how to follow required protocols while proctoring exams. As we ate lunch and took notes, we discussed the policies and concerns. But in less than twenty minutes, hallways bustled with administrators stopping at every room to inform all in charge that local police issued instructions to Danbury school officials.

Nothing was announced over the loudspeakers. Orders were quietly and forcefully given to teachers to avoid panic:

Employ lockdown mode. No one leaves the rooms, no one leaves the school buildings until further notice!

Lockdown was new and unfamiliar, but law enforcement implemented every precaution to keep us safe so, we immediately followed orders. For a while we sat befuddled but compliant. We were unaware of the catastrophe occurring in a neighboring town.

Suddenly, our visiting instructor's cell phone pinged. Rattled, she shared the news. "Oh my God! Sandy Hook Elementary school is under siege! They believe a lone gunman is on a rampage shooting school children and staff. It appears to be an isolated school, but because no one really knows, we have to sit tight and wait for instructions."

She trembled and frantically texted for updates.

Shock struck all of us. We were aware of the Aurora movie theater and Columbine High School mass shooting disasters in Colorado, but never fathomed gun violence could happen in Connecticut. Texting to families began as we sat uncertain about the future. A few were praying, some remained unusually calm while others looked overly distraught.

The phone pinged again.

"They are confirming that the principal is dead, and kids are stuck in classrooms! Gunshots continue. It's not over yet!"

Now we all trembled, and tears flowed. I was overwhelmed with uncertainty, thinking of my daughters and husband, waiting for an "all clear" and a feeling of safety to return.

Dismissal time passed. Finally, after what seemed like endless hours, we learned that it ended. No one spoke of casualties; we just followed orders. Believing the worst was over, everyone breathed a sad sigh of relief. Bells rang, and the directive came.

"Students, get your belongings and report to busses for dismissal," the principal directed over a blaring loudspeaker.

We assisted the kids and evacuated the building saying little. Adults couldn't wait to leave and feeling sick to my stomach, I rode home hysterically crying. We had yet to learn of the massive loss of life.

News quickly traveled. The shooter, a disturbed, young man, was taken down.

Many lives were lost. By early evening, television stations broadcasted all over the country: Another school shooting, a massacre of little ones and their protectors. Clips of terrified children, the lucky ones, being led to safety, streamed across the television. Kids running down the street to unfamiliar homes ran seeking safety.

Dawn Hochsprung, the principal of Sandy Hook, died blocking the intruder as she attempted to protect the young ones. I knew Dawn and her husband, worked with them previously at Rogers Park. Another faculty member, Lauren Rousseau, died defending her students. Years before, she ran track with my daughter at Danbury High. It was now personal, too close to home. It did not seem believable but became a reality when later that night, the world learned the twenty-eight names of the children and staff murdered. The deaths of children and staff left Sandy Hook residents and surrounding neighbors traumatized. We were overwhelmed with grief.

My home phone rang continuously.

"Are you okay, Missy?" Forrest asked with concern. I assured him that I was safe but shaken. "It's like a battle zone out there. These kids are crazy killing babies like that! Maybe now, they'll finally ban some of these guns."

That was everyone's hope.

After that event, the school atmosphere changed. Our school haven was rocked. We were not invincible in Connecticut. All entry doors were locked and secured. A safety official or a police officer always guarded the premises. A bullet-proof booth was quickly installed at the front entrance to deter intruders. Preventative lockdown drills, where we huddled in corners of locked, darkened rooms became normal practice, but never felt normal. Lists of procedures hung on classroom walls with copies sent home to parents. Every time we practiced, we moved seriously like soldiers preparing for an attack, praying that these drills would never be needed. It was unsettling, and I tried to reassure students.

"I got you covered. I will stand in front and cover you all. I'm Mama Nunn, mother hen and you're my brood."

Most laughed and for the wary few, I tried to minimize the danger but maximize the seriousness of drills and preparedness. I kept a rock to break windows for emergency escapes and a canister of pepper spray, just in case. Although schools should be safe havens, they were under attack across the nation.

Not much was done to eradicate the problem. Too many in positions to enact stricter gun laws spend time arguing for and against weapons, the NRA, mental illness, and amendment rights. But the shootings continue. The victims die or are forever traumatized.

Chapter 29

DURING ONE OF my final high school teaching years, twenty-three girls became pregnant! Some were home schooled and returned after three months looking sleep deprived and haggard as they juggled their schedules hoping to earn credits and complete an interrupted education. Initially, others appeared content with motherhood, parttime jobs and a temporary hiatus from education that takes years to complete. Their lives drastically and permanently changed with obligations that never disappear. I witnessed young fathers outwardly share bragging rights about virility, quickly move on and forget the consequences of their careless behavior. Many colleagues and I tried to message that choosing the mortarboard over the diaper bag inevitably afforded better opportunities.

Teachers reinforced positive behaviors, tried to serve as role models and offer alternatives to achieve endings with more opportunities and choices. I shared Forrest stories, stories of former students and sometimes shared personal stories to bring points home. My brag board, a bulletin board covered with student photos, news clippings and successes, served as a reminder of possibilities and dreams that do come true. Invited guests, graduates and even my daughters held discussion groups to prepare students for the transition and prerequisites needed for higher education.

I dangled the carrot, a degree or certification, before them, and challenged them to run the race, eliminate excuses and push forward. Like a number of my colleagues, I morphed into a personal cheerleader rooting for each child I met. Yes, it was a long haul, but reaping the benefits made the sacrifices worthwhile. Many bought in and chose education first but for some, I could not compete against the temptations outside the classroom.

Although several coworkers accepted attractive retirement packages with financial incentives that ended their teaching careers, I knew it was not yet my time. When I initially began chronicling my story, I was sixty years old. Colleagues told me that I was blessed with a youthful style and hid my age. Monthly visits to the hairdresser transformed my gray hair into a rich burgundy, my trademark. Yet, I could not stop time or the school environments undergoing unhealthy changes.

I witnessed signs and a shift in public school education. The focus on standardized testing practically replaced creative learning. Now, statistics became the new barometer to determine classroom curriculum goals. My spark was quelled as I witnessed that the new curricula no longer prioritized children first. Although there is much reliability in data analysis and it should be a consideration, not everything is measurable. I believe that test scores should never be the sole component of one's success. Many new teachers complied with the directives and followed a strict menu designed to increase rigor but minimized special teaching moments and Carpe Diem times. The new practices did not emphasize adapting teaching to learning styles best suited for each student.

"Do not reteach when students failed to understand or meet objectives. The idea was to keep moving forward and the slackers will eventually catch up."

I interpreted the messaging as: Get to the third floor without building a solid foundation. Yet, when I voiced my concern and aired my objections, I was called a cynic. I was told that remarkable growth would occur after a five-year implementation. I remained leery. They could not convince me that the design wasn't flawed and doomed to fail the students. Additionally, it did not celebrate individual student talents or staff expertise. As a result, many experienced, qualified educators chose retirement or transferred and opted for systems that still welcomed their expertise.

April 2014, I officially completed resignation forms around the same time the new system's decreasing test scores were revealed. Under the new curricula, Danbury scores plummeted just as I expected. Five years later, Danbury's scores were the lowest in the state.

I knew Einstein was correct when he stated: "Everything that can be counted does not necessarily count; everything that counts cannot necessarily be counted."

Students learn differently and cannot benefit from cookie-cutter curricula intended to improve data. They are much more than a test score.

Before I left, I shared the importance of knowing one's audience through my poetry. At a staff meeting, my principal requested I share my message.

"Student Voice"

Emotionless evaluators like statues walked into my room
Blind to the truth, couldn't see through their gloom
As they forecasted doom.
Do you hear my students' voices?

I work every night…You think I have choices?
It's either hold a job or find a store to rob
Because mom's not able
To put food on the table.

Homework can't be a priority
When paying the electric bill is up to me.
Sure, I may nod in class and want to sleep,
But feeding the family isn't cheap.

I come from a country filled with despair
I visit family and see poverty everywhere.
I used to belong, but now I'm unsure
Migrated for the American Dream, but still I feel poor.

Need a note from the doctor so my absence is okay
But no health care, I just miss another day
Absences soar like the fever I suffer
Not sure if the situation could get any tougher.

No quiet place to study or open a book
Hey, are they listening? Can they take a good look?

I'm heart-broken because dad no longer lives at home.
He's out, like a cat, somewhere on the roam. I feel so alone.
Mom works two jobs, but she still keeps us clean
And you judge us by test scores
Just what does that mean?

I think first in another language where an adjective follows a noun
I'm tested in your language where it's the other way around!
Test scores, CAFT numbers are all that they see
Won't they open their eyes to our reality?

Three months in this country and I take their test?
In my native language, I'm one of the best.
But here they examine a different score,
Make unfair judgements too early, they demand more

I see letters backwards, they smile, give me extra time
To unscramble the words...dyslexia's an issue and that's the real crime!
I accommodate, read even though I stumble
Can you imagine what it's like when each word is a jumble?

PSAT to me is a curse
I think I'll get sick, get a pass to the nurse.
Because when the numbers come back, I hide my score
And wonder what the heck I go to school for!

Do they see me?
I'm the quiet one hiding my pain. He hit me again!
I'm alone and confused. A break up, then a make-up,
But I'm feeling so used.

I'm offered class trips to Florida or Boston
I feel excited until I hear what they're costing.
Can't pay for driver's ed. to lower car insurance
Can't keep up with friends; I'm losing endurance.

Look at us!
We're the caretakers of siblings,
We package groceries and mow your lawns
We feel like chess pieces and we are the pawns.

We may wear faces that say we don't care,
Deep inside, we silently scream it's not fair.
So we buy new kicks and keep our fresh style,
But inside anger's building, starting to pile.

We're more than a test score
We just need to shout
We're running life's race,
Just don't count us out.

Take a good look at this nation
We can build bridges of communication
In this world of integration.
There should be more diversity
In each state's university
If sensitivity is what we seek
Our school is quite unique

In surrounding towns
Where test scores are high

So many are clueless about life
And we understand why.

They're frightened by difference,
By color or creed
But they All get the test score
Their colleges need.

Doesn't life experience count in what makes us tick?
We've been through so much; our skins' extra thick.

We're more than a number
And this State needs to acknowledge
It's not just a test score
That sends us to college!

So stoic, assessment statues,
Do you want to change places?
Please, remember our faces!
Don't hand us prophecies of doom
Take a long, hard look around this room.

According to your test scores
You think we're under par
That's just because you can't see who we really are.
We'll learn despite your test.
Despite the strife,
We'll soar through life
And prove you wrong.
With self made backbones, we grow strong.

You have no choice! Listen to the student's voice.

Chapter 30

LOOKING BACK, I recall when Danbury administrators assessed their teachers from eleven elementary, two middle and one high school and selected me to represent our city as Teacher of the Year in 2008.

The district administrators insisted that along with the local title, I compete for CT Teacher of the Year. The process consisted of writing seven essays on a plethora of topics, and I attempted to withdraw from the competition. But my chairman indicated that was not an option, so I followed the procedures and began writing.

The process also required two or three recommendations from colleagues who could attest to my work. All three submissions were honorable, but the letter sent by team teaching partner, Joe Vas, best described what I am like in the classroom. His words were humbling. I believe that his recommendation pushed me into the winner's circle. Perhaps this is a perfect place to share:

No one ever forgets Andee Nunn. All her students love her. Even the toughest, hardest, most streetwise teenager remembers her with genuine gentleness and care. How else could they remember Mama Nunn, who might be the coolest Mom they never had? And for those with caring, loving Moms, Mrs. Nunn was the greatest teacher you could ever have. Maybe it was the mad cool shoes, or the flaming hair or the endless funny stories. Maybe it was because she listened to the same music or recognized the same stars or shopped in the same mall. The only thing she misses is a Magic School Bus, high school edition, of course.

When I was told six years ago that I was going to be assigned a new partner to teach American Studies to juniors at Danbury High School, I was rather apprehensive. Colleagues who knew her told me that she worked well with middle school students, that she was a miracle worker, that she was "good" and that I would love working with her. I tried to contact her to arrange a meeting but, too late, she had already made arrangements to visit the high school. Turns out, she was even more apprehensive than I was. So, we spent that summer preparing our course for the year. She was a hard worker, eager to dig into the work. The grapevine was already buzzing with the news that Mrs. Nunn was coming to the high school.

The year began with a flurry of hugs and squeals of delight from almost every student who saw her. It seemed to me like she had taught every other student she met, and they hurled themselves at her with genuinely warm and joyful greetings. I grew quite used to the sound of another student shrieking "Mrs. Nunn!!! How are you?!!!" It did not help that her exuberant spray of reddish hair stood so tall or that her shoes were equally exuberant, but a lot more varied. Who could miss her? And the stories she would regale her students with, about how Macy's gave her money back because her coupons and shopper savvy actually lowered the prices of her purchases below market value. While teaching, she would launch into yet another one of her endless supply of stories (I suspect she is reaching the bottom of the well because she has actually begun to repeat them) and quickly add, for my Theory X benefit, that "it relates, honest, you'll see it does."

And it does. It always does. It is part of her magic. Her stories tell about herself and her family, but they always serve to connect her students to what they are studying. Andee is no stunted boomer, trapped in Never-never land, pretending that she is forever a teenager. Nor is she just creating a persona or a building façade for her students. She is a teacher, an excellent one, who really understands and connects with teens. She is genuine and honest with them and has no pretensions about herself. Her students love her for it. When she talks about her hair appointments, she lets them know that she understands how important it is to them to look right, to present proper appearances and to respect themselves. She has just the right touch when she tells a young hip-hop fan that he needs to pull his jeans up and not expose his underwear. She can tell a young lady, quietly, that she is extremely well-dressed, but perhaps a top that is less revealing would be more appropriate for school. She likes their music but also lets them know that trying to listen while in class is unacceptable. She asks them to read their poetry in front of others and she shares the same. She shows them that they can be themselves without compromising high standards. As for the shoes, well, we all have our quirks.

By the way, most of the time, she teaches too. She makes all her lessons live. It does not matter what she teaches, she will make it sing and dance, literally. When the students read The Great Gatsby for our unit on the 1920s, she taught them to dance the Charleston. When we studied the 1950s and '60s, she brought in music she listened to when she was in school and taught the students her dances. When we read Death of a Salesman, she had students identify critical scenes in the play, rewrite them to change the outcome, and act them out. The students were thoroughly engaged and never forgot the critical elements of the play. When she taught vocabulary, she made sure it derived from material that we were studying and often concocted the strangest mnemonic devices to help students remember them. I have met students who had her in sixth grade who still remembered words she taught them.

Mama Nunn's specialty is successful with "challenging" students. She works as well with students returning from jail as those headed to Yale. Students who would never pick up a book avidly read anything she puts in front of them. She knows just what to do to hook them. She makes it a point to find literature that speaks to them, and she makes sure that she connects what they study to their lives. She reads to them; she reads with them, and she makes them read. She encourages them, supports them, and never lets them feel like they are not good enough. No other teacher I know can call a sullen six- foot four student "cookie-face" and have him eating out of her hand.

Mrs. Nunn rarely has to discipline students. Students who are engaged have no time to act out. She has little tolerance for disrespect and meanness. That is when students knew the sterner side of Mama Nunn. She will accept no slurs, no unkindness, and no rudeness. I recall a particularly heated classroom discussion on race and social class in which students were trying to express strongly and passionately held views. It was a difficult conversation, but she had taught them well, by word and deed, that such discussions need not descend into hate and vitriol. It was impressive to watch teenagers control their passions and yet express themselves with conviction.

At the end of our first year of team teaching, we decided to have a small closing "awards ceremony" for our class to give out small awards to students who showed superior achievement during the year. Typical of Andee, by our second year together, she went on a massive shopping spree, and now we have a big "AWARDS CEREMONY." She called me at home to tell me what she had bought for whom. She has actually accumulated enough leftover gifts now that she has to store them in a large packing box, the kind used for international corporate transfers. How could she have done anything less? She loves all of her students, especially those most in need of it. She does not just give to them at the end of the year. Quietly, throughout the year, she gives them clothes and food. She visits them at home and in the hospital when they are sick. She puts needy children in touch with help. She and her husband have even established a scholarship fund for deserving students. Truth is, she gives of herself.

No one ever forgets Andee Nunn. All her students love her. It is not the shoes, or the hair, or the music, or the stories. It is her. She loves her students, cares about them and is honest with them. She is mad cool, as they say, but she is a trusted adult with standards and values that she expects them to live up to. For her students and those who teach with her, she is not only Teacher of the Year, but a very significant person in their lives. She does not need a Magic School Bus.

Sincerely,

José M. Vas

Social Studies Teacher, Danbury High School

(Thanks Joe!) Frankly, I believe his flattering letter catapulted me to the semi-finalist position.

Following instructions, I forwarded the letters for evaluation and before long, two envelopes from the State Department of Education came. Inside was a congratulatory note accompanied by an assigned date for a personal meeting in Hartford for the CT Teacher of the Year interview. The panel enjoyed my essays, and I was selected as a semi-finalist for CT Teacher of the Year with a final assessment interview to follow.

I was proud but nervous. Yet my two best fans cheered me on.

"Honey, you earned this. All those kids you touched; our whole town knows that."

"No surprise, Missy. You learned a long time ago how good you are."

So, with Ronnie and Forrest's words, I traveled to our state capital for the final phase.

I was not awarded CT Teacher of the Year. My Hartford interview sealed the judges' decision. With a panel of about twenty-five educators sitting in a raised U-shaped semi-circle looking down upon me, I answered questions honestly. I felt like a fish out of water with a physical appearance quite contrary to the educators before me. But that was not my problem. I knew I adored my students, learned from them, and that messaging was apparent.

My obvious lack of advanced technological skills caused my elimination. I was not computer savvy enough as the Internet took over. My younger competitors were more computer literate and ready for the online future. In the end, I breathed a sigh of relief because I did not want to take my teaching on the road, lecturing to other faculty groups. I wanted to remain in the classroom, go home to my students.

But that was 2008 and after a good run, I left fulltime teaching and opted for an adjunct position at Western Connecticut State University where I had worked in the early nineties. I could change hats, teach college students, and have freedom to adapt my syllabus. This was a positive choice for me because I still had much to do.

Memories and ideas filled my brain. This change could allow me more time to gather my thoughts, write, reflect, and communicate with Forrest and other students who kept in contact.

"Good for you, young lady! Pass on your ideas to the ones moving ahead. Make them new mentors, new leaders and keep on keepin on! You're not my Teacher of the Year, You're my Teacher of the Century!" Forrest chuckled.

I did not doubt my decision to keep moving.

"My Finale"
It's not you
Not your style or unique smile
Not your size or the color of your eyes

It's not the way you walk or talk the talk
Not your hair or what you wear
Not your voice or mannerisms at all
Not your size: big, tall, or small
It's NOT because of you I say goodbye

It IS because of you, I remained so long
When I felt defeated, you made me strong
You gave me purpose to stay on board and fight the fight
You gave me hope; you were my light

It started in Brooklyn with Forrest, one of you
Who showed me what I could do
In a classroom filled with lost souls whose hearts were yearning, burning
For information, respect, attention, and learning

He passed the baton to Laurence Fishburne,
my student who at age eleven
Transformed himself on a junior high school stage
Starring in "Hurdlin'", my original play, before he became a Hollywood rage

It was you, Sonia Almonte whose passion for art
Became a part of a plight to teach
as I helped her reach… her goal.
In Darien, my Dominican is the school's diversity!

It was you Leighton Roye, my joy or Luis Rodriquez who made my day
with smart responses only he could say
Or José Pimental teaching History and naming his babies after my family
Or English teacher Jana John my student at Rogers Park
whose sweet smile helped to spark… my creativity

It was you, Jomaly Duran winning the battle with cancer
Simultaneously teaching me lessons in courage and perseverance
Or Luis Pantoja and Hugo Raposa, medical students
working to cure the ills of society
Health is their first priority.
Or Evelin Garcia, living the Dream Act today
A Harvard graduate, she's on her way.

It was you, all of you from around the globe
who kept me here until I grew old
Speaking your varied languages, sharing your cultures,
teaching me something new each day
You, the sea of faces before me, made me stay.

It's Special Friends, teachers like Agnes, Hourani, Lieberman,
and many others who make it so hard to leave.
And my "school Husband" Joe Vas, my special partner and buddy
who for eleven years made me study- History
FYI: there will NEVER be a team like us, not because they decided to erase
American Studies from this place
but rather because our oil and water mixed perfectly
And, because what we shared is remembered
in the lives of those we taught

It's not my husband Ronnie or my two daughters who heard all of
your stories and listened as I shared, because they too cared
Or my smarter sister Max who still edits my writings about you.
I hear each voice, listen to each story
Your lives filled me with empathy and glory.

But now times are changing, and teachers are rearranging
Their lessons to follow new rules
Redesigning the purpose of our schools.
Increase the test scores; watch the data
I believe much more should matter
Let's not increase rigor and
Eliminate creativity and uniqueness.

To the designers who reinvent education do not forget
that students and teachers cannot be cloned.
It is unreasonable!
Teachers need to make you want to learn in any way feasible
It could be tragic, to eliminate the magic that stirs imagination.

As I close this curtain, I am certain
I'll see some of you at Western where my creative flair will still be there
where I can tell a story and stray from the lesson
Because it makes sense for me to do so without worrying about closure.

It's not any of the thousands of students I taught
for over 40 plus years that bring tears
They are my treasure, my pleasure, my non-
biological babies embedded in my memory.
I record your faces, your names, so precious to me
No, it is not you; it never could be

This is my sunset
As the new wave floods the system,
It's time for me to get out of the water, so

With a sigh, I say goodbye and
Thanks to each student and every friend
Who joined the adventure until its end.
I do not regret, I will never forget… my journey.

Chapter 31

ALTHOUGH JULY 2014 began retirement from Danbury public schools, I was not ready to permanently leave the classroom or store all my materials, including original lesson plans that worked well. I was not ready to feel obsolete.

My intension was to continue working as an adjunct teacher. For three years prior to leaving the public school system, I had taught one late afternoon communications class at Western Connecticut State. I hoped to teach two classes to keep myself in the classroom sharing knowledge with older students. Most adjuncts worked day jobs and were unavailable to teach morning classes so, to my delight, the chairperson granted my request for two sections, and I accepted Monday and Wednesday back-to-back morning sessions.

I had new ideas to bring into the class and ran many thoughts by former students and Forrest for feedback. I wanted current, relevant issues for students to research and debate in my decision-making in groups course.

"Don't use the same old stuff, like capital punishment," one remarked.

"Talk about existing problems like admission policies occurring on campus," another suggested.

"Use criminal justice stuff or racism or gender issues, subjects that affect their generation. You gotta get them, Missy. Get material that's current and speaks their language. They're the next group of voters, so make it all matter."

I took heed and spent the entire summer researching, writing, and reworking a syllabus before sending it to the department chairperson for approval. My topics were controversial and could generate conversations for students to express their opinions. I was excited, especially after my syllabus was approved and I was given permission to run the course as I chose.

I called Ronnie who was not surprised when I shared the positive response from my chairperson. "I did it!"

"I knew you would be successful. With your experience, this is a piece of cake for you. You worked all summer. Good for you!" He sounded proud.

Then I called Forrest. "Well Missy, here you go again. Out to make more magic."

My new life changed my schedule. I set the alarm for 7:30 even though class commenced at 9:25. I learned early in life from my mother, being early was a positive asset. I arrived early to grab one of the limited parking spaces closer to the building and to use a library printer when necessary for handouts. Although I distributed much work online, I elected to use paper hands-outs for classroom material. The goal was to learn how to work with others in solving issues, finding compromise, and adapting techniques to help listening and delivery.

My classes were mostly freshmen with a sprinkling of upper classmen. There were a few reluctant seniors, still terrified to address an audience as their anxiety heightened at the thought of an oral presentation. I discovered, however, regardless of the age difference in this setting, I needed to listen to my students, again to hear their stories. Initially, I believed that because the population was older, their problems would subside, they had beaten the odds. As accepted college students, they already achieved a certain level of success, and they could coast carefree through their educational journeys. I was wrong in my assumption.

Isaac

August 2015, I received paperwork from student services regarding a young man enrolled in my course. The information provided detailed accommodations necessary to meet his needs. So, I adjusted not only curriculum guidelines and due dates, but I also adjusted my approach. Having previous experience with Asperger's syndrome, a type of autism, I would become less aggressive and more observant. I learned in the report that he struggled with written assignments, obsessed over topics at any time and needed constant verbal direction and reassurance. I was ready for the challenge but never expected some of the behaviors and talents he displayed.

Day one, he arrived, sat front seat center row and with little volume control, introduced himself to me and the other twenty-three occupants in the room. Reactions from peers varied. Some smiled or chuckled and were immediately aware of his limitations, but others rolled eyes impatiently assuming this new guy to be a thorn that needed to be plucked. That first day was challenging as ice breakers permitted students to share and learn about one another. Isaac shared a long-winded story about going on a cruise. He emphatically announced his refusal to wear a life vest during a routine drill on board. He repeated this again and again.

"I don't need to practice. We will never use those boats. I have been on many cruises before."

I made the mistake of explaining the importance of following rules, but this caused him to emphasize over and over again, "If it isn't a real evacuation, I don't need not wear the jacket!"

He was adamant. His peers, on the other hand, groaned and grew impatient.

After time, his monologue temporarily ended, but after dismissal, he approached me to argue the same point. He persisted to discuss the issue that plagued him. I found it difficult to reroute the discussion. For four consecutive class sessions, I redirected conversations that reminded him of his boating incident because he was ready to again echo his objections!

But other events made him endearing. During one group assignment, where peers worked in triads, I juggled listening and advising group members so that students could fill the requirements successfully. Sitting next to Isaac, I explained the instructions using hand gestures as I spoke. Without thinking, I touched Isaac's hand and instantly, he retracted it like he was touching a hot stove. Realizing I had invaded his space, I apologized and explained that my light touch was an endearing sign of friendship. Then I changed the subject and returned to the assignment. Within five minutes, I felt fingers touching my wrist. Isaac was staring at me looking for approval as he broke a barrier himself. It was a special moment.

The following week, he invited me to join his family at the cemetery for a special service dedicated to his deceased father whose life ended too early. "Mrs. Nunn, do you want to come to the unveiling for my dad?"

He knew I understood that a year after a soul departs, a veil is lifted from the gravestone as the official mourning period ends in the Jewish faith. I gracefully declined and explained that it wasn't my place to share the intimate moments with his family yet, but that I was honored to be included.

That satisfied him.

I also smile remembering the results of that creative advertising assignment. His group invented a spray to combat body odor. The original product came in unusual flavors so that, for example, if used in November, one could be sprayed with "turkey and stuffing" scent and in October, one could choose "pumpkin". As he advertised the product, he then proceeded to overspray one of the group members completely coating his partner with air freshener. The class roared, most laughing at him while a select few enjoyed his antics.

Still, despite my mission to get others to respect and appreciate Isaac, most shunned his friendship. In one last opportunity, Isaac proved how talented he really was. Knowing about his special gift, I privately asked him to bring his violin to class and play a tune for us. Isaac was a virtuoso violinist who played classical pieces, as well as original work.

He sat first violin chair in numerous orchestras, including in college. He agreed.

The following Monday, Isaac arrived with his violin ready to perform. I informed the group of a special treat.

I introduced Isaac who chose to perform an original piece he recently completed. The audience sat stunned and speechless as Isaac's melodic performance filled the air and touched a few hearts. Then applause rang through the room, and he bowed robotically, paused, placed the instrument in its case and returned to his seat.

Finally, peers witnessed his uniqueness and understood that the socially awkward boy who processed differently and sounded odd, possessed an abundance of musical talent. Many thought twice before mocking and berating him again. A few were teary-eyed like the teacher.

He graduated as a music major in May 2017 and continues to perform.

Robert

During a spring term, during a problem-solving assignment, a student openly shared his story about having a Percocet dependency. As a mandated reporter *and* a concerned professor, I spoke with him confidentially and referred him to the Drug Counseling Center. Rob followed my suggestion, but he visited the center when it was in the process of a leadership change. New directors took over, listened to his story, and either passed his case on or put him on hold for too long with no resolve.

Weeks later, the counselor finally addressed his issue and recommended residential inpatient treatment. He insisted upon parent involvement to review any available medical coverage. Rob demanded no parent involvement and at twenty years old, believed he could make decisions without involving his family. As a response, the counselor delayed finding solutions.

He completed my fall course earning an A proving that regardless of his condition, he was smart.

A year after I met Robert, I opened the following (unedited) email… enough to devastate a teacher:

Dear Professor Nunn…

Hello, it's been a while since we last talked. I guess I just wanted to say a few things and got no one to talk to. I just wanted to say I wish I listened to you and the resources on campus.. Things for real outta control. i couldn't get 'high' off pills anymore so i switched to heroin.. started using a needle and what do u know.. i been to detox 2 times, tried suboxone, now I'm going to rehab.. I'm not sure why I'm writing this and tellin u but wanted to tell you, if u have other troubled kids, u can tell em u can't quit alone, its just impossible.. it's been 11 days since my last use and I'm still withdrawing bad.. the last year alone, i took out the maximum in student loans (roughly 6500) and that wasn't even when I was in your class.. I've sank to the bottom, stole from my jobs, my family.. damn this is no way to live, I'd say since January, I've wasted over 10 grand and lost the trust of everyone i know.. i just wish u the best of luck bcuz u were one of my favorite teachers.. actually the only one who gave a damn.. i wish you the best and i don't know if i will get back to using this email until next year.. (i'm goin to rehab.. then my mom's taking me back to China until next year, to get my mind back to normal before i come back to CT) .. anyways .. wish you the best !

R.

Shocked, I responded right away with words of concern and encouragement. He left the country without a word until a second email arrived.

Professor Nunn,

I apologize. I received your message way earlier but I was not in a good position so did not feel like I could reply back then. Also sorry for the following improper grammar - I haven't had a school course in so long, I kind of just got lazy in sending messages and emails.

The truth is, I just wrote a long message to you just now, but deleted it because I don't really want to scare you on how bad things got, so long story short -

For now, I am taking it one day at a time. I quit all the drugs that were illegal but kind of directed myself toward legal drugs I can buy at a local smoke shop or head shop. It's not nearly as bad as before so I am managing, but a quick overview.

I stayed in China about two years. Got back to the states and moved to Houston Texas. For now, I got a full-time job and still trying to put things right with my family. It's still a struggle every day, I have no friends down here (which i don't mind) so it helps a lot with not going out and looking for bad influences. Because sometimes I just want to go ask random people that look bad if they can help me find a drug or something like that, but I haven't yet so it's good. I started my job 2 weeks ago so I'm trying to save up money to pay my mom back for all her help and maybe save for my own vehicle and eventually save for what I want to do in the future. I just have one more hurdle, if I can't get over that, I can safely say I feel normal.

I'm glad to hear your still teaching Communication courses. You were one of the best teachers I ever had, period. Teaching methods, keeping the class interested, and caring on a higher level than almost all other teachers. I hope you enjoy your retirement. I do apologize, I'm not sure how to reply correctly. I just hope you are happy in the end. Thank you for the kind words and encouragement. I hope the past semester went well for you and I hope you have a great summer. I will keep in touch.

I responded but sadly, did not hear from him. I tried again and again to no avail.

Every year, students faced tragic situations that interrupted their studies, but they marched on. They shared their stories with me in emails, in assignments and in person. I ached for them.

- One woman lost her brother to a drug overdose and needed a week off to grieve with her family. Her mother refused to store Narcan in her home.

- Another's mother lost her battle with cancer at age forty-five. I attended the wake since I knew the student from high school and again, as she sat in my college classroom. As she coped with disaster, I minimized her workload after realizing that this was the second parent she lost since her dad died when she was in elementary school.

- A third fragile, young woman who previously apprised me of her inability to cope with her bipolar diagnosis and constant medication changes, arrived in class unprepared, donning black sunglasses asking for a moment of private time outside. There with tear-stained cheeks, she shared the news that over the weekend, her fiancé committed suicide after a major argument between them. Since he had no living family members, lawyers reached out to her regarding the twenty-eight-year-old man's funeral. A week later, overwhelmed by guilt and responsibility, she dropped her semester's course load. She reregistered for the following term hoping to be stronger by the time the new semester commenced.

- An Israeli ex-soldier, a class leader, shared stories of war and the fact that her partner was still jarred by fireworks and loud noise that brought flashbacks of bus explosions on the streets of Tel Aviv. Together, they battled the trauma of war and additionally, faced rejection from families horrified by their same-sex marriage. Raising a young son, they depended only on one another and some special friends after being denied family support.

Chapter 32

DURING THE SUMMER of 2019, the new department chair mistakenly changed my teaching responsibility and scheduled a different course, interpersonal communications, for the fall term. Feverishly, I spent endless hours in June, July and August creating a viable curriculum and ventured into a different domain. Even after so many semester openings, so many years, I felt unsteady, a bit skeptical although I over-prepared. I opted for no quizzes, no tests. Journal reflections, group projects, short papers, individual presentations, and numerous opportunities to speak filled the requirement list that I announced on day one.

Most celebrated no exams, but many were unsettled about speaking although this was a communications course. So, I welcomed the chance to change them into better communicators and provided a wide range of eye- opening activities for engagement.

The rosters exploded. There was a waiting list for entry into both sections. My chair approached and asked me to override the maximum and permit a hearing-impaired student ready to graduate but who had avoided the communications requirement. Although the additional student threw off group numbers, I agreed, and the recommended woman accompanied by her language signer joined us. I made sure to adhere to her accommodations, and we instantly enjoyed each other.

My class began with a daily bulleted outline listed on the white board to structure the day's events. I never assigned work that went unreviewed.

I never just lectured. During each session, students moved around, watched film clips, collaborated, shared read-outs, and voiced opinions and ideas. Happily, I witnessed total engagement, lack of cell phone interference and minds at work. Even the sign language assistant participated in the group activities. The atmosphere was upbeat. Ninety minutes flew by. The term began well.

I tried a few times that August to contact Forrest to boast of my success, but he was unreachable. I knew he had a late summer birthday, so I wouldn't give up even though he wasn't returning my texts or phone calls. This was not like him. I even wrote on his Facebook page wondering about why I was suddenly being snubbed. I waited.

Then his wife called. "Good morning, Mrs. Nunn. Forrest asked me to give you a call. It's been a tough month for him. He suffered a heart attack a few weeks back and with his diabetes complications, his kidneys are deteriorating. He requires ongoing dialysis."

She took a deep breath and continued. "The Florida Veterans' hospital was ill-equipped and unable to provide the necessary treatments, so he was transferred to a VA hospital in Georgia. I'm on the road now looking for an affordable rental to be closer to him."

Before I could respond other than gasping, she provided a contact number for me so that I could speak directly to him. "He would like that," she affirmed.

"I appreciate your call. Your family is in my prayers, and I will call him today."

"Well, all morning he is busy with treatments, so wait until after lunch when he is back in his room resting. That would be better for him."

Of course, I agreed. I was rattled and ashamed that it took me so long to investigate if anything was wrong rather than assuming I was being ignored. Right after lunch, I dialed the direct line to his room, and he picked up after two rings.

"Hey, friend, are you enjoying the attention?" I kidded, knowing he would avoid a serious conversation.

"Hello young lady! I hear you've been looking for me!" He sounded upbeat and pleased.

"I gave the family quite a scare. But frankly, I enjoy kidding with lots of cute nurses and getting well, thank you very much!"

"You mean flirting, knowing you," I retorted.

"Haha, no one knows me better. I tell you what, Missy, I'm losing all that extra weight and gonna be ready to break hearts when I jump this place."

We laughed and talked for about fifteen minutes until he sounded tired. "I better go, they gotta get me hooked up to this silly machine again. All part of the program."

He appeared more annoyed about the inconveniences rather than concerned about his illnesses.

"Well, follow orders and do what they tell you. Too many folks need you to get well and go home. I'll call you again in a few days. Still worry about you and love you."

"I certainly hope so! Yes ma'am. This is an army hospital, so I gotta follow orders." He laughed and hung up.

When I tried his line later that week, there was no answer. I assumed he was undergoing treatment and tried another day after class to no avail. A few days later, my house phone rang.

"Hello Andee. I am on my way to the hospital and thought to call you and tell you myself."

It was Forrest's wife pausing and attempting to gain composure.

"Forrest passed last night. He suffered a second heart attack and did not pull though. He was very frustrated by the dialysis but trying so hard to cope with all this. I think it got to be too much and he lost the fight. I wanted to tell you myself that he is finally at peace."

His wife sounded rational and calm, but I broke down, overwhelmed by the news. I tried to thank her for thinking of me and apologized for my incoherent response as my voice broke. I think she understood but she did not go further. We ended the conversation. That was it. Too young, too early. He was gone.

Hysterical and heartbroken, I sought comfort by leaning on Ronnie. My husband knew how important this young man was and he attempted to console me. I was mourning the loss of a dear one whose impact never left me. I knew I would keep him permanently alive in my stories.

I returned to work thinking about how often people judged Forrest without ever getting to know him. They stereotyped the poor, angry Black kid as big trouble. I decided it was time to investigate how deeply stereotypes affect our communication with others.

When I assigned the Harvard Implicit Bias Tests and required written reaction responses to their individual findings, the dynamics in class changed. For some, results were unsettling. Forced to address overt and hidden truths, many became aware of feelings that often needed to be personally addressed while a few doubted the results, believing that muscle memory controlled their responses. But for the majority, the exercise brought a new understanding about ingrained behaviors that, if confronted, they could be altered. They learned much about cultural differences and how preconceived notions often direct behaviors. It was a good lesson, led towards empathy and ways to right the wrongs they witnessed or practiced in the past. Hopefully, they carried the lessons outside to friends and family, demonstrating how once truths are exposed, misconceptions could be addressed. Maybe they would think before pre-judging, a lesson I learned from an eleven-year-old "gangsta".

When the term ended, I felt triumphant as students' reflection comments rated the course exceptional and verbalized positive reactions about what they learned. I loved the subject and waited to repeat the experience for the Spring 2020 classes.

Spring brought a unique opportunity. Traditionally, Western served mainly Connecticut locals, usually commuter students who juggled educational obligations and work hours without time to socialize much on campus. Costs for in-state students made higher education a reality, but on-campus residency primarily housed athletes, exchange students, honor students and a smaller number who opted to live on campus because of less feasible commutes. Now for the first time, Western offered in-state tuition to applicants from both New York and New Jersey. The new initiative with reduced tuition was enticing and attracted students from surrounding states who, under the new guidelines, could afford to live on campus. Also, the number of New York day travelers whose commute was doable increased. It was a win/win as the administration's goal to make money and provide more on-campus activity was underway. Many more would opt to spend weekends at school rather than commuting home. The climate became more exciting as new faces from different places filled the classes.

Until Spring 2020 term, I enjoyed the ride. But drastic changes occurred about seven weeks into the term when COVID-19 struck the country. I completed one day of training for online teaching, took copious notes and left overwhelmed by new directives. After posting mid-term grades, as spring break neared, on May 16th, the university officially closed. Dorms were emptied and sanitized. The campus looked like a deserted ghost town. We entered a new era when virtual teaching commenced.

When a worldwide pandemic invaded our lives, the web saved the day. COVID-19 isolated us and for many, socialization occurred only over the Internet. Of course, virtual learning and its Zoom sessions made connections. For me and my course, however, it could never substitute for human interaction. New issues and new challenges arose quickly.

That began my downfall.

No matter how computer savvy one was, virtual instruction challenged everyone. Although we tried to stay in compliance, students and staff battled illness at home; some became caretakers for siblings and elderly family members. Whether implementing special grading programs like Blackboard or Grade Book, meeting with students on Zoom or Google doc. or any of the plethora of packages available, chaos reigned.

Personally, I never mastered the Blackboard program in my one on-campus beginner instructional session. While I understood some of the basics, even with my notes at hand, I failed to remember all steps to follow and easily became confused. I revisited the site several times before feeling totally defeated. Instead, I implemented an alternative, a weekly Google doc that reached everyone.

Both instructors and students faced daily pressures as we became innovative and determined to complete the term. Despite the long-distance learning, I tried to include timely and interesting selections to continue engagement and successfully get through the semester.

Policies changed often as administration juggled ideas in an attempt to resolve issues, find viable solutions and save the term. They offered a pass/fail option to ease frustration. And even that was a mess! Some believed pass/fail could be applied to any or all courses, but the message, often misinterpreted, seemed to differ from case to case. The wording was misleading to most of us. One student chose to use the P/F choice for only two courses, but the administration elected to change all his classes to P/F—no exceptions permitted despite my urgent pleas of support. The student who earned an A in my class received credit only despite letters validating that he spent most days visiting his disabled twin brother hospitalized in a non-COVID hospital wing. As many others, he misinterpreted the policy guidelines. Unfortunately, because of ever-changing mixed messages, the administration refused to add the A. Decisions were not refutable.

Every student passed my class. There were the few C grades, nothing shocking, but there were many improved pieces as students persevered and mastered the concepts. A few noted that they were eager to enroll in my other course for the following Fall 2020 term, but they were in for a surprise.

My teaching career was over.

My awakening came when I learned that fall semester would not return to normalcy, but rather, a hybrid solution: one day in class, one day online. We understood that in the event of a second outbreak, the university would return to online classes only at any moment. Since I thrive on face-to-face, in-class teaching, I declined the offer and conveyed my decision to my chairman.

So, I sigh, and remember the thousands of faces and stories that fill my brain, the wonderful memories that fill my heart. I am no longer a cheerleader for learners, but I thank them for the lessons they taught me.

I continue to share their stories as a tool, a critical component for understanding difference and critical race theory, as well as an avenue to invoke empathy and respect.

The Magic Show

"A piece of writing is like a piece of magic.
You create something out of nothing."

—Susanna Clarke

I CAN ONLY call my students' musings and expressions of the deepest parts of their lives while growing up in my classes, *magic*. Some could barely read a word or speak English as they approached my first assignments and questions with timidity at best. But their willingness to learn, dig within, push to create, and share honest portrayals of home life and identity cast a spell on me that would never break. I wish I could publish one each from the several thousand students I had the pleasure of teaching and knowing. Here is but a sampling of the magic, with permission by the authors to reprint. I have changed some names respectfully.

FORREST

I am the fourth child of two loving parents, born in the Bedford Stuyvesant section of Brooklyn, New York. Although I had three siblings that came before me on this earth, I am the first male child of those parents.

I guess the neighborhood I was born into was a decent one, where everyone knew each other, where families looked out for one another. It was a working-class neighborhood. This was the only thing I knew; I was much too young to remember, but I guess it was a dangerous neighborhood as well. My father worked in a glass factory in Brooklyn, while my mother was a stay-at-home mom, the typical late fifties, early sixties type of thing. I still remember going on family outings, rides in the car, picnics, and barbecues even though I was only two and a half years old. I can remember running in a botanical type setting with my father chasing me always saying, "When I catch you…" and since I didn't know what would happen when he caught me, my little legs would run as fast as I could, although it never seemed to be fast enough because he always caught me. Every time he did, he tickled me until I cried or wet my pants. I remember one time being chased and caught by my father with him swinging me around until I pooped in my pants. Boy, I recall my mother giving it to him as she was the one who had to clean me up.

Soon after that I can recall my mother and siblings sobbing uncontrollably, my mother's sisters and grandparents coming over to comfort them, In fact everyone was crying. I didn't at the time understand what was going on, all I knew was that my father was not there helping to console my mother or my siblings. However, I do recall never seeing my father again. It was not until years later that I found out what everyone was crying about, you see that was the day my father was murdered. I do not know what the circumstances of his death were, I've only been told that it was a violent death. What a blow, a woman with four very small children with a husband who was here one moment then gone the next, a father whose life was snuffed out on the violent streets of Brooklyn, New York and only God knows why. My mother did everything she could possibly do to make life normal for my siblings and me; church became a driving force in our lives. Other family members would pick us up and take us places. They were doing any and everything they could to help, but they, too, had families of their own.

My aunt was a den mother with the Cub Scouts of America, and she took me to meetings until I was old enough to join. I remember becoming a member and being given my first uniform: blue pants, shirt, and hat along with the yellow handkerchief that you wore around the neck with the Cub Scouts of America emblem all over the uniform. I just knew I was hot stuff then. I can remember marching in parades with the throngs of people lining the streets waving and me waving back with a smile. There was a pee wee softball team that I joined, and we played softball games with other kids in various parks in Brooklyn. Although I don't ever remember winning a game, it was still lots of fun. There were trips to an amusement park in Brooklyn called Coney Island, Palisades Park in New Jersey, Bear Mountain in upstate New York. I remember playing a game called skelly, touch football, stick ball; these were all games that you played in the street. Those were the happiest days of my life. I would have loved for my father to have been around, but that was just not how things turned out. My heart pains to this day wondering what should have been or what could have been, if only I had a little more time with my father.

My first day of school was another milestone for me. I remember crying like there was no tomorrow because by then I had become a mama's boy, not having a father around. It was the first time being on my own not around other family members or my mother. I guess I was like most other children, a little scared at first. I remember being told I had to grow up, to become the man of the house and an education was part of becoming a man. Back then I thought they were just tricking me, yea right, a boy becoming the man of the house, so I swallowed the line and went to school. I made friends very fast and then I just couldn't wait to get to school. Those first years of elementary school were fun for me. My teachers made learning fun, and for some reason or another, they always showed an interest in me. I was always called upon to answer questions, seeing that 99% of the time I gave the answer correct, I was given extra things to do, and I did them with a smile. Homework was never a problem for me because for me, I would always go on vacation just by reading a book. They always brought me extra things at school that would help expand my horizons. I remember one teacher even started me on a stamp collection. (I had a whole lot of stamps- if I only knew where they were at now, wow!) I loved going to school and everything appeared to be alright at home, I was always smiling, not having a worry in the world: I had a good life then.

The fifth grade was another good, but scary year for me. I knew I would be leaving that school and going to junior high school with much bigger kids. My teachers, seeing that I had a lot of anxiety about the transition, helped build my confidence by telling me not to worry, that I would be okay if I stayed on task. Believing them, I started looking forward to junior high school.

That summer, my mother had to take a job, I guess to make ends meet. Working all different types of hours, I was left with a male babysitter and that was when my world was turned upside down, never to be the same again. It was awful without having anyone to tell. I decided that I didn't ask to be here and said to myself, what the hell. That's when I began this very destructive behavior. During that summer, I began running away from home, riding the back and sides of buses, riding the back of trains. That's right, the outside of moving trains, stealing from stores, stealing cars, fighting just about every day. That was the summer I was transformed for life, being hit in the eye with a car antenna in an attempt to rob somebody. I didn't care because I thought no one cared about me. I said, "Fuck it, I didn't ask to be here." I became a very angry person not trusting any adults. People in the neighborhood always warned that the things I was doing were very dangerous, but once again I didn't care. Remember this was the same neighborhood that took my father.

Soon, I was arrested and placed in the juvenile home. I was a little scared at first. I remember this one kid trying to bully me. I recall not doing anything at first, then he tried to take something of mine. I knew then I could do one of two things: let him take it and become a victim for the rest of my life or fight, so I chose the latter. In fact, I whipped that kid's ass choosing to never become a victim.

When I arrived back in the neighborhood after being confined at juvie for about two weeks, I was treated like a hero within my peer group. You see I was the first to be arrested and sent to a home and, for me it was no big deal, I didn't want to be at home anyway. I came back with my chest stuck out daring anyone to mess with me; they never did. The older teenagers tried to put us nine-, ten- and eleven-year-olds back on track by giving us this stupid nighttime curfew, where if they caught us outside after a certain hour, they would beat our asses real good. I was caught once or twice, and they did just that. Some more of my friends got caught with the same result until we just got tired of having our asses whipped, so we turned the tables. We would group together and go out searching for them individually.

And once we caught them, it was their time for an ass whipping and they got one just as severe as they had given us. Before you knew it, every night we would have "sham battles," that's what they were called. Fighting with the older teenagers was just great, lots of fun as long as you didn't get caught. I remember being arrested again that summer, being sent back to juvie, with that same kid who was there the first time, still there, only this time I bullied him and everybody else, for everyone remembered me from the first time. I fought at the drop of a hat- no big deal, that's how you got respect, and I earned my share.

The summer was almost over, and I was headed to sixth grade, but prior to being released from juvie I had to see a judge. In a stern voice, he told me that as a condition of my release, I have to go to school and stay out of trouble. Of course, I agreed just to get out of juvie and return to my bad ass friends. When it was time for school, I kept my word I went to school. I just didn't stay, that was not part of the conditions for my release. I went the first time for two full days, but I just wanted to run the streets. It was on one of those two days, that I met what I thought was this real cute white teacher who would later become a major influence in my life. I noticed her, however at that point, I didn't trust any adult figure. I didn't want anything to do with school, so I never went back until months later that first year becoming a truant and hell raiser. I just wanted to continue living the same bad ass lifestyle that I had chosen. Remember, I didn't care because I didn't think anyone cared about me. I didn't ask to be here.

It was during this time, after all the sham battles and being put out of the house, our small group became first three then ten, then twenty, then fifty and before you knew it, there were one hundred and thirteen of us and we called ourselves 113 Hellcats; that's when the real terror began. I was a full-fledged juvenile delinquent in all its glory. We stole like there was no tomorrow, we robbed people, stole cars, just for the hell of it we stuffed phone booths all over the city. We traveled to other neighborhoods just to terrorize them, no big deal, that shit was fun, the only fun we knew.

I was arrested for the third time and sent back to the same old juvenile home, but this time it was different the faces had changed. I had to prove myself all over again. I remember two boys tried to jump me, but you know me, I just wasn't having it. I remember fighting one and when I started to get the best of him, his partner jumped in. I had to deal with him and though I was tired as hell, I was still battling. When his buddy recovered, they both came at me. I was no fool. I remember picking up a chair and just swinging, and before it was over two kids had their heads busted open and I was placed in a cell for the remainder of my time there.

What can I say about isolation? It is designed to make a person think about actions, to let you know that your actions/behavior is not tolerable. It's an effort to get a person in lockstep. However, other rules exist, although they are unwritten. They are understood by persons living that sort of lifestyle and the first rule is survival. You do whatever you need to in order to bring about a bearable change in any given situation and you worry about the aftermath at another time. You have to give yourself an advantage by any means necessary and you can apply the same rules to those streets today. So, in order to control my situation, I sang. Yeah, I sang all day, into the night and I sang loudly. I actually liked the echo the bare room provided because there wasn't much to absorb sound. All I had was just a steel bed frame, thin mattress, commode, and sink. I watched annoyed guards peer in on me through a small window to the hallway and I knew I beat the system. Nobody would break me, not even in the lonely, boring cell at "Camp Juvie." Oh well, I got that much needed respect.

Prior to being released this time, I had to appear before the same old judge whom I believe was a little pissed off at me because he heard what I did to those two kids. He asked if I had gone to school… I didn't lie, I told him I had, I just didn't tell him how many days. I remember giving him this bullshit line that I really enjoyed school and I missed being there and couldn't wait to get back. To my amazement, he released me once again under the same cond'tions: go to school and stay out of trouble. I thought to myself, damn that was easy. It was at that point; I just lost all fear of the court system and what would happen if I was ever arrested again. I went to school for about four short days, until lunch and would haul ass just before recess was over.

"I Did Not Ask to Be Here"

It's tough out there; I don't really care.
For no one really cares about me.
I never asked to be here in this world,
with people who walk around as though they
have blinders pretending not to see me.
I DO EXIST.
I'm mad as heck!
I don't get any respect.
Why?
Is it because you think I don't have anything to say or is
it because you just won't take the time to listen?
I needed you yesterday, where were you?
I need you today, where are you?
I will need you tomorrow, where will you be?

Remember, I didn't ask to be here!

Can it be that you are so consumed with yourself
that you have just forgotten about me?
Am I supposed to find my own way?
Do you think all you have to do is give me a little food?

Infested boxes of cold cereal, "shake before
eating" to make the bugs flee,
Post Sugar Crisp, browned puffs of wheat, swallow
with an occasional camouflaged roach.
Do you just tell me "shoo" and think I will just go away outside to play?

Remember, I didn't ask to be here.
OK, I think I understand.
I am really on my own.
My only usefulness to you is that government check that
you wait on every month, maybe twice a month,
I don't know. All I know is that I didn't ask to be here.
I need your protection, I need your nurturing, I need your guidance,
I need your love; I need you to show me the way.

Remember, I didn't ask to be here.

It appears that I have become a burden,
One that you just tolerate because I AM here.
So, with that being the case, I'm gonna just leave.
I don't know where I'm going or how I will get there,
But I'm going even though I'm scared.

Remember, I didn't ask to be here… BYE!

The first couple of nights I slept on a park bench, only to be joined
by some friends who didn't ask to be here either. So, we made a pact,
one in which we all decided that we would look out for one another
until our dying days. Without any skills our first order of business
was where to find food. We had no money and I refused to beg or
borrow, so I stole that first meal. Some Suzy Q's and milk; I thought
to myself, gee that was pretty easy and it was also exciting and
before I knew it, I was a thief-a pretty darn good one at that.

After the excitement of stealing wore off, we started stuffing phone
booths by sticking wads of paper in the coin slot. Peoples' coins
would get stuck and when they would press the coin return nothing
would happen. Thinking they just lost their money, they would simply
walk away, and, at an undetermined time, we would come along with
a piece of wire, stick it in the coin slot and money would just flow like
from a slot machine. After doing that all over the city, some days
we collected forty or fifty bucks. Wow! That, too, was exciting.

On days we were unable to tap the phone booths, we would play games
of chance like craps or see lo (dice games) although it wasn't a game
of chance because we knew what would happen if either of us lost; we
would just take all the money back and dare you to do something about
it. Most times people would do nothing and for those who wanted to
challenge us, the fight was on and oh, by the way, we never lost a fight.
In fact, some people wound up going to the hospital. Our reputations
grew and before you knew it, instead of it being a pack of three, it
was ten, then twenty, then fifty and when the final tally came in,
there were 113 of us and we called ourselves the HELLCATS, terrorizing
our neighborhood and other neighborhoods just for the hell it.

Although all 113 of us very rarely hung out together, the core group
of ten managed to stay together all the time. Riding the train all
night, carrying "Saturday night specials," 22s, beating up and
robbing people, suctioning to the side of city busses for a free ride,
I was so out of control that I had been incarcerated at least eight
times. It would have been more if they could only catch me.
The few times I did get caught,
They always wanted to beat me with things like
extension cords, fishing rods, pipes, sticks.
You get the picture, anything they could get their hands on.
So, I ran.
I ran as fast as these legs would go, some time for miles.
And when I didn't want to run any more, I would
steal a bike and ride for miles.

when I got tired of riding the bike, I would steal a car.
That didn't last very long.

The police caught me and beat my ass.
One arm cuffed to a steaming radiator,
My right arm wildly swinging back.
The police beatings weren't too bad though.
Because I had been in many scrapes before.
In fact, almost lost my left eye in one of these battles.
Fighting with car antennas,
Eye blinked at moment of impact.
Eyeball rolling, muscles tearing,
The scar that I wear, I didn't care.

I was only nine and I didn't ask to be here.

EVA

"Finding Freedom: The Story of an Albanian American Girl"

As I proudly sit here waiting to graduate, I think back on my life and what brought me to this moment.

I was born in Albania. I am the oldest of three children, the daughter of V. and VC. Until the age of eight, my family lived in a small town where we were exiled from the rest of society. Since my family spoke out against the Communists, they suffered and were punished for their political beliefs. We also did not have freedom to worship freely. Communism did not allow us to worship our religion!

In 1990, students rebelled and took over the government. Finally, Albania became a democracy! My family was able to relocate and live freely. We thought our lives changed forever. We were able to practice freedom of religion, attend private schools and colleges, open our own businesses, and not suffer discrimination. But we were wrong! This peace did not last. Even though my country is beautiful with many good people and pretty places, Communists chained us when they returned to power. My family decided to run away. We lived in fear for two years while armed Communists had the power.

Finally, on October 29, 1999, I left my country filled with tears, hoping for a better future. I felt broken hearted because I did not want to leave my old life. So, I arrived in America as a pessimist. I did not know English; I had no friends; I was a stranger. It took me a whole year to change my attitude.

Special people helped me to become who I am today. Today, I am optimistic about my future. Many different influences helped me become successful.

First, thanks to my family, my mom and dad who left their homeland so that my sister, brother and me could have better lives, lives filled with opportunities.

I will never forget my Uncle Eddie who worked so hard to bring the family to America.

Special people and teachers at Danbury High School taught me not only English; they taught me about American life and customs. They made it easier for me to become an Albanian American girl.

And finally, what a special country we live in! America offers me a place to enjoy freedom and peace. Sometimes it is hard for me to think that there are some people who want to destroy the freedom and peace of this nation. Even though the evil of September 11 stays with us, this country did not fall apart! We stood together knowing what we stand for is right!

American never forgets all people! It offered the people of Albania a home because this country continues to fight for other people's freedom and peace.

In the words of country singer Lee Greenwood:

I thank my lucky stars

To be living here today,

Cause the flag still stands for freedom

And they can't take that away.

I am proud to be an American!

KEVIN

"Semper Fidelis"

In the ten months of nineteen sixty-nine that I was alive, I was living the life of an angry, young, Black infant. My biggest concern was a dry, odor-free diaper. I was working on building my vocabulary from goo- goo to mama; Khe Sanh wasn't even in the formula.

I was raised by my mother, who was too young really to have an understanding of Vietnam and its far-reaching implications. Her biggest concern was keeping me fed. My mother was aided by my grandmother and great grandmother, both of whom knew that Amerikkka did not give a "gnat's nipple's" worth of care when it came to the Africans in this country.

At that time, my biggest fight was in the high- chair with my mother, who insisted I eat strained peas over my most fervent protests. This day-to-day survival was paramount, not the violent storm brewing in Southeast Asia. My father was off doing his own thing. At seventeen, he had one more year of high school, and colleges were "looking at" him. He made it into college and did not die as so many of his friends had. He's a success, but other than that, he is nothing more than a footnote in my history.

I carry the anger instilled in me by the wisdom of my great grandmother who taught me that if the disrespect and mistreatment prevalent in her childhood are still being practiced, that nothing has changed. There was a cousin of mine who went to Vietnam, but he stayed in the Army for twenty years, so there was no opportunity to ask him about Vietnam or related politics. That is one problem with the Black race; we have very few living testimonials to bridge the gap between what is truth and what is said.

I was born on the west side of Stamford, Connecticut, into the loving arms of a young, gifted, and Black mother. I can only tell of things I carry from the 'hood that were mine. I had my own Tet Offensive, and the Hoods had their own D.M.Z.'s where one could still get hit by The Bloods in the Hood carry all the love and hate and every emotion in between with them into the day to day.

This was a time when an African's life was not considered worth very much, and the fact that I was a boy decreased its value. I had an Uncle Andrew who was shot in the throat by the police, handcuffed and bled to death while they tried to figure out how to handle the "situation." He was sixteen and Ho Chi Minh meant nothing to him. Stamford's westside taught and gave me through attrition all the things I now carry. It was its own self-contained world; it had stores, a center, and a park. The hospital where I would later work was right up the hill. The only thing that it did not have was a school near-by that I could attend.

There were, of course, drugs and all their related problems. There was a knowledge that "selling" was wrong, but in my hood, being broke was a bigger wrong. I learned that the biggest branch of the Heavily Armed Forces and outright criminals was the police. Along with the badge came the license to steal and to disrespect anyone of color regardless of station. So, you see, it was heard to give a *&9o! About the My Lai Massacre where you are getting killed by inches.

It was not by any stretch all misery. I learned of the creativity that comes without having the monetary foundation necessary to thrive in Amerikkka. I was surrounded by some of the most gifted, talented, witty, funny, scary, and violent people to be found. The park was a hot LZ. Of song, dance, and athletic endeavors where a word could lead to anything from marriage to funeral, compliments of the Downer Funeral Home.

No matter how far I go, the hood follows. I received word that a friend I grew up with was kidnapped a few weeks back under some dubious circumstances. When Spring break came, I went home to see my mother who told me that they found Jeffrey's body in New York mutilated. It bothered me because we grew together, stood side by side. The simple fact was that enough of the brothers in my hood died already and only so much mourning is permissible lest it soften your resolve to fight for your survival. I'll go to another funeral on Tuesday and be playing basketball by Wednesday; that's the nature of the beast. Is that Post Traumatic Stress? Maybe it is, but there is this saying: "Yeah, though I walk through the valley of death, I shall fear no evil, cause I'm the baddest motherfucker in the valley." That's how we lived and still live because we knew then as we know now that all you ever had, all you'll ever have is your soul and only a soft foolish punk would let anyone step on his soul.

Even though we were scared naive children, we would perpetrate with a mask of hardness until it became real, and you were left hardened. The Brothers philosophized about God, and the majority of us came to the opinion that God does not seem to live in low- income housing. We discussed the fine art of wooing or, to be more precise, dipping our wicks. Hell and heaven, that's what we had in the hood. The White Man was just a transient presence at best, at worst he was an occupying force. We were never at eye level. This was kool with us; this was our world. He had fucked up everything else. We did not need him bringing his rhetoric, his propaganda or his damn wars into the hood be they Vietnam, El Salvador, Desert Storm, or the most popular and ambiguous ones—the wars on drugs and crime. The White Man wants you to see and feel his tragedy, both foreign and domestic, to feel and understand his pain. All the while, hoods like mine all over die by inches and in some cases, blow up. So, you see, I give less than a damn about Vietnam, other than being sympathetic to the loss of life. It is hard to give a damn about those who don't give a damn about you. That was life in The Hood; we grew up as a family, dysfunctional as it was, and I as just one of the boys in the Hood.

KRISTEN

This is the introduction of what makes me the person I am today. My name is Kristen, I'm a girl who's Brooklyn born, but was raised in the Bronx. From what my mother has told me, talking has never been an issue for me. Starting from a toddler, to elementary school, to high school, I've always been an outgoing social butterfly and was probably the easiest person you can talk to. Athleticism, sports and competitiveness were all second nature to me and especially during my teenage years, it became my get away when I was going through a rough time or needed to get my mind off things. There a lot of things that people wouldn't know about me or what makes me the way I am today unless they grew up with me during middle school. My life from the ages 11-13, I'd say had the most effect on me and my personality.

Yes, I was and still am talkative, friendly, and outgoing, but back then, who I was on the outside didn't portray who I was on the inside. I grew up being made fun which caused me to have a low self-esteem and a lot of insecurities. Everything from wearing glasses, having short hair, being one of the tallest girls, wishing that I had a lighter skin complexion at one point, all took a toll on me. If there was a way to change something, for example going from wearing glasses to wearing contacts, I tried to make that change. The sad part is that everything I tried to altercate was more in search for the acceptance of others rather than me accepting myself. Although, this is how I felt on the inside, I managed to mask my emotions and act like nothing was wrong. Whenever someone made fun of me, I used to laugh along with them so it would feel less like they were laughing at me. It's not like I didn't have friends who already accepted me, but I wanted to be the person who was everybody accepted. I had a hard time recognizing the difference between people who were using me for their benefit vs people who genuinely wanted to be there for me because I was naive and had too much trust or people who didn't deserve it.

Halfway through 8th grade I got involved with someone who I thought would've been my first boyfriend and he just so happened to be one of the more popular guys in my school. For a girl who had low self- esteem, it's almost like I felt honored to be looked at differently and everything I was trying to change about myself was finally being recognized. To make a long story short, a few weeks into conversing with and getting to know him more, he invited me over to his house. Being that I was 13, I was also at the stage of wanting to have more freedom than what my mother gave me, but I knew she wouldn't allow me to go to a boys house after school so I told her that I was going to a volleyball after school. When I arrived, I soon found out that we weren't alone.

Again, me the being naive, overly trustworthy, young-minded girl that I was, I had trusted him with my body. I immediately regretted having the slightest bit of trust in him when I saw he had three other friends in his room. I felt so uncomfortable and disgusted, I instantly tried to get away but it was four against one and I was defenseless. By far, the worst Friday afternoon of my life, and to make matters worse, I find out Monday morning that there was a recording that went around over the weekend. The bullying that I was going through before had gotten 1000 times worse after the situation occurred. Some girls were persistent with wanting to fight me and didn't give up until they got the reaction they wanted out of me. I've been punched in the face, had books knocked out of my hands with bread thrown at me, which cause pigeons to surround me as I picked my books up and I've even been pushed into the street as traffic was moving. I absolutely hated my life and couldn't wait for high school to get a fresh start. You never think that stuff you hear in the news are capable of happening to you, but if it does, how do you handle it?

Everything that mattered to me at first such as wanting to be accepted and trying to please everyone no longer mattered to me. Granted, having to retrain my morals and thought process took a while but the change of scenery when I went to high school and got the fresh start I needed definitely did help along with the assistance of my mom and guidance counselors. Although high school wasn't the easiest road either, the improved mindset I had allowed me to stick up for myself and not be afraid of anyone. When I first started school in CT, I went through the same issue the first few weeks of wanting to be accepted and wanting to be everybody's friend but I quickly realized that I was done trying to change myself to meet the requirements of others.

I taught myself that it's okay to say no to people and anybody who can't accept no for your answer doesn't deserve a spot in your life. Not everyone will be accepting of me and I'm at peace with that because at the end of the day it's their loss and my benefit because the smaller the circle, the less drama there will be. My personality has gotten a lot more bold and outstanding since then and my inside now reflects who I am on the outside. Any altercations that I consider making in my life are all for my benefit. To this day, there are still times where I feel the need to speak out on another's behalf who's being bullied on. It still triggers my defense mechanism and something I'm still sensitive to. Being that I've become such an outspoken person, I am now working on learning to pick and choose my battles. Realizing that there is a time and place for everything and even then, I have to be aware of what I say, how I say it and who I'm saying it to in order to live more of a stress- free life.

NASIR

I always knew that I was queer, odd, from being the only caramel-mocha colored child in a predominately Caucasian pre-school, to preferring the simplicity of nature compared to the action of Super Mario Bros. But in sixth grade, I really knew that I was queer. Not just artsy, but very different than the average snot-nosed sixth grade boy. I guess the epiphany erupted when I pranced around my house to Madonna's "Vogue" and noticed the male eye-candy in her flamboyant music video. Madonna and other divas from the 1980s, like RuPaul, urged me to embrace my misunderstood creativity and to try drag.

A stiletto is the only item that has held me back from being successful. In the backroom, the sequins gleamed in my face as I visualized my performance. I repeated to myself, "Step, kick, turn," praying that I would not forget. While chanting, I prepped my face. I applied the creamy foundation and blush. I dazzled up the eye area with a metallic colored shadow. I then applied red lipstick to bring a dramatic effect to my visage.

The first half of the gender bending process was complete. I dressed myself in a wine red, laced corset. The daunting task soon appeared: trying to fit into a pair of scandalous hot pants. I jumped up and down, threw myself against the wall, and sucked in my gut until I could zip them up. Despite the war with the pants, I gladly slipped my size ten man feet into a size twelve pair of women's stilettos. To complete this glamorous look, I placed a vibrant, multi-colored wig on my head.

To distract my mind from the horror of performing in front of four hundred college students, I focused on the material of my stilettos. I analyzed them, concluding that, although they were appealing to the eye, the cheap material was starting to irritate my feet. The emcee interrupted my thinking train when he announced, "Let's welcome Vamiculas to the stage performing Lady Gaga's 'Bad Romance'. My heart stopped and shyness shadowed over me. After teasing the audience with my leg peeking through the curtain, it hit me that I was performing in drag for the first time!

I burst through the curtains and fiercely began lip-synch to the top 40 hit. My intent- earning the title "Best Queen". Ignoring the unstable stiletto, I pranced around and smiled directly towards the judges. Profusely sweating, the last thirty seconds of the song approached. Insisting on a memorable finish, I intended to complete a spin and pose, but instead, I managed to spin, slip and almost fracture my ankle in the fall. The crowd's gasp magnified my embarrassment; I limped backstage in agony.

Sadly, I did not earn first place and I assume that my accident lost the honor. I scolded myself, felt like a failure until the idea of performing hit me again. I obviously entertained the audience, so why did I fret over a tacky sash? Pondering over its significance, I realized that not being perfect did not make me a loser. My Payless stilettos and my infamous fall is a prize for my passion and my ability to be honest with myself.

Nasir entered Manhattanville with scholarships and grants that would pay for his college experience. He continues to be true to himself and explore all the possibilities for a content and exciting future. Already completing internships in his field, during spring 2016, he began a study-abroad program in France and is living his dream come true. He traveled all Europe and continues to seek adventure as he absorbs knowledge about the world, its people and finding the right niche where he is embraced. Many of his musical ventures can be watched on YouTube and are quite entertaining.

CHANTHIP

"The Journey"

I have always had a rough childhood. I did not have the choice to go outside and play with friends. I always had to help out around the house and do chores. Just my luck, I was born into a poor family. Also, I am the first- born child and my parents were disappointed that I was born the wrong sex. They were hoping for a strong boy who could bring food to the table and support the family. Every day they reminded me how disappointed they were, that I was a useless girl. They never appreciated anything I did; they just complained and felt sorry for themselves. Then, one misty morning, something happened to my village that affected our lives completely.

We were in the field planting tomatoes and peppers when my aunt came running towards us. I never saw her run so quickly, as if she was running from a ghost or something. She went directly to my mother who was planning pepper seeds into the ground, but when my aunt whispered something to her, my mother dropped everything, and her face turned colorless. For a moment, I thought she, too, had seen a ghost but when I looked around there was nothing and besides, it was the middle of the day. I was ordered to return to the house and fix lunch, told to be quiet and do whatever she ordered. Immediately, I cooked rice and boiled vegetables. We could never afford beef or pork- too expensive. Come to think of it, I could not remember the last time we ever had steak and peppers for dinner. I did not want to interrupt mother and aunt still talking outside but if I waited to tell her lunch was ready, it would get cold, and she would yell at me either way. I approached; they stopped talking but I could feel the tension between them. It made me uneasy.

Why wasn't I a boy? It would be much easier and maybe, I could solve their problem. I sat arguing within about feeling hungry, selfish, and worthless. My mother soon walked to the sink, washed, but her trembling caused her to drop and break a glass. When I questioned her, she shut me down and told me to mind my own business.

Later my father came home. I always admired father, a strong soldier who served his country and protected his family. Soon, I overheard them talking. Mother was crying, begging my father to pack and leave, but he refused. He was born in this country, lived in this country, and wanted to fight for this country even if it cost him his life. The Khmer Rouge was going to invade our village…. that is what aunt had told mother. What did we do to deserve this? We never stole food or hurt anyone. At that moment, I realized that there was nothing I could do to help my parents. It did not matter if I was a boy or a girl, there was not a single thing I could do.

Part 2

In 1975, the Khmer Rouge invaded Cambodia and took the law into their own hands. Many people died from starvation or were killed by the enemy. My father, a soldier for his country, a patriot, died fighting for his family and country. My family was captured and entered a concentration camp with many others from the village.

We were fed only one bowl of rice soup a day per family. Those from large families often fought for food. In my case, it was mother, my sister and me. My mother only drank from the broth to keep us alive. When she could not bear the torture anymore, she led us from the camp, and we escaped. We walked endlessly and managed to reach Thailand. In 1981, we emigrated to the United States, the land of freedom.

In a foreign country, my mother found it hard to adjust to the new environment and language. My mother, Deng, grew up with Cambodian customs and traditions. Growing up by age six, she was working in the fields and contributing to her family. She did not enjoy a childhood like American children. Her marriage was arranged, and her life was planned. Here, in a strange land, she could not adjust alone. By 1984, she remarried a Cambodian man and before I knew it, I had one half-sister and one half-brother. Being the oldest, it was my responsibility to care for them both.

My teenage years were not enjoyed like my friends. I had to stay home, clean, cook, complete chores, and baby-sit. Only on special occasions was I allowed out, but only with female friends. Even now, as a nineteen-year- old college student, I still need permission and usually argues with me before I attempt to leave the house. It seems that I cannot please her; I am never quite good enough. She never appreciates the many things I do for the family and finds something wrong with whatever I do.

I am the first in the family to attend college, but it causes more stress. Now I babysit, run errands, work part/time and attend classes. I have little free time as I try to find myself in this busy existence.

JOMALY

"I'll Be Fine"

Simple cold, at least that's what I thought,
Doctor visit, emergency room
25 tubes of blood, two chest x-rays, MRI
Final analysis, bone marrow and spinal tap
Back aches, headaches, visits from people that I love
Nurses checking my vitals every 10 minutes, sleepless nights

Disgusting Hospital food and smells
Backless pajamas, messy hair, decent looking room
Final diagnosis…Leukemia
Wow! One look at my mom, two minutes of tears
"Suck it up", I tell myself
I'll be fine
Two surgeries, bruised up arms from all the
needles, an IV machine following me
Expert on my so-called sickness
Acute Lymphoblastic Leukemia
Common in Hispanic and white teenage females; I
was one of the many lucky ones I guess
Go home for the weekend, telling everyone about what has happened
I smile they cry
Surprised stares, "why do bad things happen to good people"
I'll be fine
Long chain of prayers, New York, New Jersey, Boston, Florida, Georgia,
Connecticut, and Dominican Republic, wow, I feel so loved!
Monday morning, you all wake up for school
Monday morning, I wake up for chemotherapy
Insert needle in my chest and head
Weird colored liquid going into my body
Five different types of pills to take home
I'll be fine
Feel so out of it, not in the mood for anything
This isn't me
Short hair, so pale, nervous hands, swollen face, dry
skin, brittle nails, weak legs, losing weight
It seems month passes by, no school, boredom hits home
Lay in bed looking at the ceiling; it's so exciting
I'll be fine.
Still no sleep, I'm like a walking bladder, bathroom every hour or so
Praxair Cancer Center, my second home
Three times a week, I'm considered the baby there: "only youngin"!
Make jokes with the nurses while she pokes my finger

White blood cells don't even show up, red blood cells extremely low
"Wear your mask, no fresh fruits or vegetables, stay away from colds"
I'll be fine
Weekend is here, you all go to the movies, mall, and parties
Weekend is here, I lay in bed looking up at the ceiling
Check in with my doctor; ask for permission to go to places
"Wear your mask", he insists "and no funny business with boys!"
End up going to a sweet 16, try to dance and get tired after 2 songs!
Everybody having fun, I sit and smile
I'll be fine
Weekday begins once again
Normal routine being dragged on to complete another day
Tutored by my regular teachers for an hour
Try to concentrate
I can't even write without getting a cramp on my hand
I stand in the door listening to my nephew cry
Can't hold him without my arm having what looks like a seizure
Stomach growling like crazy
Can't hold a plate without almost dropping it
I'll be fine
I'm 16 years old, Dominican; born and raised in Brooklyn, New York
Last year nobody knew who I was
Today I'm known and loved by a lot of you
I'm an optimistic person
I'm not popular, or perfect
I mean who wants to be!
I'm extremely happy being just like every dreamer in here
My name is Jomaly Duran
I have Cancer
And I'll be fine

M.

My birth mother relinquished her custodial rights to me when I was only a few days old.

After signing her rights away, she returned to her apartment in Dolgoye Ledovo, Russia, where her mother, her boyfriend, she and three other children resided. As she returned home, I stayed at the hospital abandoned with no family. After a few months, I was transferred to an orphanage an hour and a half away from my hometown where my family was happily living their lives without a clue of my whereabouts.

I lived in the orphanage for eight months before being placed into a family in the United States.

As years past, I never questioned my past. My parents always told me I was adopted from Russia, and I never questioned it, so they never gave me the details of why. I was and still am a happy girl. I grew up in Southbury, Ct. in a loving, nurturing home with my parents and adopted brother. They gave us everything humanly possible.

I was reserved, quiet and never wanted to be the center of attention. Terribly shy, I clung to my mother and for a long time, I would wallow if left alone with some unknown person that wasn't her. I was very attached, possibly an unhealthy attachment, but it was never much of a concern until I entered primary school. Maybe my body and mind subconsciously knew about being rejected causing my problems with communication.

I became attached to other primary caretakers, drifting towards teachers rather than making solid friendships with peers. I sat next to the teacher during story-time and even have a first- grade picture standing next to her holding onto her arm.

Throughout school the anxiety worsened. I had a fear of rejection, spent time with one friend rather than socializing in group settings and hated large gatherings like dances or parties. But time passed and as I entered college, the tension eased. I became more comfortable with my new way of life but started to question my past.

Who was my birth family, where am I from? Does my birth mom

ever think about me? I approached my parents who then shared my adoption information. Excited to discover I had three older siblings somewhere halfway across the world, I began a search for them. After a few months, I located my oldest sister, Alena who initially rejected me thinking I was a fraud. Eventually, I found my older brother Yuri and my other sister, Svetlana. My birth parents would not respond to my inquiries even though they know of my existence and are still together.

Yet, finding my siblings has helped me communicate my thoughts in words. I ask more questions and generally am more verbal without feeling shame. The timid girl is becoming more comfortable and developing a voice of her own."

"COURAGE"

My student's assignment was to describe a problem and how she would go about solving it.

1. On April 13, 2018, I was raped on campus and since then have developed PTSD.

2. Not only does it affect me, but it affects my friends, family, significant other and even strangers I meet.

3. It is very serious right now as I am in the process of getting a single room on campus because of my panic attacks, insomnia, inability to eat and reoccurring nightmares. It is very strange that sometimes I don't think about it at all and then there are other times I shut down and think that something irrationally horrible is going to happen. I think about it every time I get in bed to sleep, every time I get a bruise, every time I see someone who looks like him, every time I get drunk and sometimes, I think about it out of nowhere.

4. The cause: I got extremely drunk one night, started hanging around a guy who seemed nice. I passed out and woke up the next morning in severe pain, covered in bruises.

5. There is no solution to the problem but there are things that help.

After it happened, I went to the Women's Center where I got some help, and they brought me to the hospital to have a rape kit done. That was the first step to help myself. I knew how controversial rapes can be, but I knew what happened to me and I was determined to prove it. I sat in the hospital 6 hours being pried and prodded.

6. Two days later, I moved out of the dorm where my rapist also lived. Then I brought my mother to school, showed her my new room, and explained why I moved. I brought her to my advocate in the women's center. She had no words, but I no longer carried the burden by myself.

7. Next, I tried to fill the hole inside, so I started sleeping with others to find comfort. Of course, this had the opposite effect on me. By the end of the term, my mother made me see a therapist twice a week hoping to crack my hardened exterior and have me reveal how traumatizing the event was for me. But whenever the therapist tried to talk about the rape, I shut down and said nothing. My doctor increased my anxiety medication to the highest legal dose and all my emotions went out the door.

8. In June, I decided to press charges. I filled 5 double sided pages- a timeline of exactly what I remembered. I filed the paperwork, submitted it to the judicial committee, had an appointment, went into the car to drive to the meeting and stopped cold. I couldn't get myself to do it. I didn't want people to look at me differently and for some reason, I didn't want to ruin the rapist's life. So, I just continued therapy 2x week.

9. When I arrived at school late August, my anxiety skyrocketed. I tried to pretend it never happened, but it haunted me everywhere I looked. Three weeks later, a roommate arrived, and my brain started messing with me. The insomnia started, I couldn't eat, panic attacks daily, shaking, throwing up and my body shut down. The doctor increased my meds and added Xanax. I filed for an emotional support animal because of the severity of how I felt, my PTSD. No solution yet, but I am taking steps do hopefully, one day my mental state will improve. I do not have control yet. I am blunt, type A, very straight-forward but my brain isn't working rationally.

R.

Both of my parents immigrated to this country from Uzbekistan, formally a republic of the Soviet Union. My dad's family was originally from Armenia and mom is from Russia. They met going to college in Tashkent, capital of Uzbekistan and came to the US right before the collapse of the Soviet Union. My brother and I were born 4 years later. My parents knew no English when they came here but enrolled in English classes when they arrived. For a few years we lived in Brighton Beach, Brooklyn which was and still is a predominately Russian-speaking section. We later moved to Ossining and then to Shrub Oak, NY, a small town at the northern border of Westchester County where I spent most of my formative years from age 7 until completing high school.

Growing up my parents did not teach us Russian for reasons still unclear to me. They wanted us to be well adjusted to American life and feared teaching us Russian might hold us back when it came to learning English, which I grew to understand. An extended family member's son had to enter ESL classes, so maybe my parents had a sort of foresight. They did not want me labeled ESL which could limit me in classes. Also, there wasn't a large Russian community in Shrub Oak or surrounding towns, so I spent most time in English speaking communities. It is a strange dynamic that my twin and I spoke English as our first and only language. Although my parents speak English fairly well, some conversations are mired in misunderstanding and confusion. They get the wrong idea and I have to reexplain. I never seem to have trouble understanding what others say and I pick out important bits of what someone else might say. Sometimes I am too verbose when fewer words could suffice.

I became good at understanding people with different accents. My dad owned a lunch counter-type restaurant in Yonkers and for years I worked with him. One customer said the owner, my father, had a thick accent which I never realized- I was just accustomed to it.

Sometimes people think I am standoffish, too harsh, or direct or honest. My parents never sugar-coated anything, maybe due to a lack of vocabulary to find words to make a message more palatable. Maybe that is why I sound the way I do. Sometimes I just keep my mouth shut so I am not proven wrong, or I do not sound like a know-it-all. Other times, I talk about things I know little about just to make me seem smarter to others. I think I just have to listen to what people say instead of assuming what they will say.

J.

I was born in Peru. The majority of my life growing up has been in the United States. I was raised in a household with one older brother. I have played the violin in middle school and high school. Since I was little, I was raised in a Christian household. I love playing sports, especially soccer. I enjoyed watching soccer games and playing at the park with friends. Since elementary school, I've been humbled to be raised in a household that has taught me to priorities education more than anything. I have been in the honor roll from my middle years to my high school years. I am fluent in Spanish and English which has come in handy in many ways. Throughout my life, I have had experiences that have shaped me into the person I am today.

Accustomed to speaking Spanish at a young age, elementary school was a challenge to adapts to. As I enter the classroom on the first day of school, I watched as all eyes in the room focused on me. Nerves began to travel throughout my body. As I stood in front of room, the teacher introduced me to the rest of the class. All that I was able to do was to wave and say "hello" due to my language barrier. Quickly, I walked to the seat in the back and tried to avoid attention. Students sitting around me would introduce themselves to me, not knowing that I had no clue what they were say. I tried to communicate with others with the minimal English I knew, but all I would get in return were giggles. I felt embarrassed because it felt as if they thought I sounded funny. Feeling embarrassed I just slouched in my chair and hoped for the day to be over. The bell rang and it was time for recess. I was scared at first because I didn't know who was going to hang out with. As I entered the playground, I looked around hoping someone would approach me. Luckily, someone did. Someone who would be one of my closest friends. His name was Maurizio. He was just like me. He introduced himself to me in Spanish. In that moment, I didn't feel alone anymore.

When I was growing up, I would always watch my brother has he would leave the house with soccer cleats in one hand and a soccer ball in the other. Around the time I started middle school, soccer wasn't something I was interested in. I preferred just running in general, but at a young age I wasn't allowed to run by myself. Noticing that I spent too much time at home, my mother told my brother to take me with him whenever he leaves the house to play soccer. At first, I wasn't interested in going, but the curiosity of what my brother would go, won me over. When we got to the park, my brother told me to play with the younger kids who were playing on the other side of field. I walk to the other side of the field. Timidly, I asked the group of kids if I could play with them, and kindly responded with a "yes". Excited, but nervous at the same time, I played defense and tried to avoid the ball as much as possible. Trying to avoid getting passed the ball, I would stand quietly by the side of goal. Sadly, it didn't go as planned. As the ball rolled quickly towards me, I tried to think of a way to control the ball. Without any solution, the ball bounced off my shin rolling a meter away. Quickly, I ran towards the ball trying not to give it away to the other team. As I approached the ball, I notice another player running towards the ball too. Quickly, I lunged my foot to win the ball. Unsuccessful, I missed the ball and painfully collided shins with the other player. I laid on the ground with immense pain from the huge bruise on my shin. After that day, I wasn't able to walk for a week. Ironically, that incident made me love the sport of soccer even more.

Religion has been an important aspect in my life. I am a Seventh Day-Adventist. Since I was little, I was taught at Sabbath school about stories of the bible and the ideals I should follow throughout my life. My beliefs have shaped me into the person I am today. From not stealing, or doing drugs or alcohol, I believe that I would've been a completely different person without my beliefs.

The biggest challenge of all that I have faced in my life is living as an undocumented immigrant in this country. Up until my sophomore year of high school, I lived in this country illegally. My parents had to work jobs that paid them the minimum and supported the family enough. One of the problems of not having any legal documents was that health insurance was not an option. I remember at a young age, I would have a fever, but sadly, not having health insurance, my mother had to take care of me the best she could. She would stay awake all night looking after me, knowing she had to work the next day. When the program DACA was passed by President Obama, I felt a sense of hope because it opened doorways that had never opened for me for the majority of my life. This program allowed me to get a job, health insurance, my license, and most importantly a college education.

Overall, all these experiences have shaped me into the person I've become. I get nervous whenever I stand in front of an audience. I've learned to always try to make new friends because there could always be a person who's new and is too afraid to introduce himself to others. Religion has shown me to be respectful to others and appreciate everything I have in life. It has taught me to be a vegetarian. Being an immigrant has given me the chance to work hard for everything I want to accomplish. It has taught me that giving it your all will always be rewarding. Most of all, it has made me appreciate my parents the most, and given me the opportunity the give back to them for what they've done for me since I was little.

CIERRA

As a young child into early adolescence, I devoted much of my time to practicing martial arts. This, along with the strict parenting style of my father, played a huge part in shaping my life and who I am today. When I was only eight, I achieved my black belt, and when I was 12, I received my second-degree black belt. I was held to super high standards and pushed to be the best by both my dad and teachers. My grades were near perfect, I was even required to bring my report cards into karate practice. I got recommended and accepted into the Summit Program, for "the gifted and talented." In karate, I was a star of "The Dream Team." I was used for every example, in karate class and in regular school. When I hit middle school, the pressure started to eat me alive.

Too fat, too smart, too ugly, not cool, not a part of an extremely financially stable family. A/B on a paper? Embarrassing, I was told it was disappointing and that I could do better. And I knew I could, but why should I be so stressed over one stupid grade? There are people out here who are actually suffering. With real problems. I had it good, right? Ignore, suppress, distract. I thought about space and beautiful places unexplored until I got so overwhelmed it brought tears to my eyes.

It went on like this for most of my teenage years. I quit karate, and started smoking pot as soon as I went into high school where I I picked up volleyball, it's a family sport and my father was friends with the coach.

"Hi, I'm Cierra and I play volleyball…"

And that's about it. I sit here and look pretty, I guess. I had a boyfriend who I would spend most of my time with, we had fun. I broke up with him eventually because I did not think he actually loved me after about two years, same with the next boyfriend who I dated for almost 3 years. I was treated as an item, but I know it is up to me and my power to express how I deserve to be treated. People will pick up on how you view yourself. And I, I was supposed to do as I was told, don't try too hard, don't fight with your brothers, be cute. High school relationships are stupid anyways, but it kept me occupied.

I hated school. I hated the system. I hated the mundanity of my life every day. I smoked pot every day. Starting in middle school, I sometimes went to sleep as early as 7pm. I still couldn't get out of bed in the morning. But some nights, I just laid there and tried to push out thought after thought of regrets. That C I got. The time years ago the karate teacher left the room for a considerably long amount of time and the class was expected to hold a pose. I slightly followed a fellow classmates lead and released my pose for A FEW seconds, dramatically less than everyone else. Still however, when the teacher returned, he called out the class and said, "Be like Cierra, she held the pose the whole time," and I was frozen. I couldn't tell him, even though the whole class saw me take a significantly shorter break than they did. And then I recall, my parents saying they were going out to grab milk and coming back hours later. Where were they? Fighting over money, fighting in general, cheating, in therapy?

On a positive note, I was a fantastic babysitter, super responsible and gained A LOT of experience. My younger brother is 7 years younger than me. And my older brother is 7 years older than me, although he wasn't around much and has a different mom. He went to prestigious private schools and wound up at Boston University with a considerable scholarship. Jokes on him, because he'll be paying loans long after I finish paying mine and wandering around with an English degree. I'd never say that to him, I love him, but he has a way of speaking to me and taking away every single victory and diminishing all pride and achievements I think I have made.

Never. Good. Enough.

I understand where he's coming from now since his mom was a crazy control freak and I'm sure the way he spoke to me is the way he also treats himself. So, in a way, we could say it's out of love, even if he doesn't always know it. He just wants me to do better, even when I've already done amazing. He knew all my buttons and exactly how to push them. When I lashed out at him for it, I was the one reprimanded by my parents. When my younger brother would break into my room and vandalize it and destroy all my toys, again I was to show NO temper whatsoever. His artwork on my walls was praised. It was pretty good I can't lie, but he drew a life-sized SpongeBob one time which stayed there for over two weeks before my mom helped me clean it off.

I was really close to my dog who died when I was in 7th grade, and that was my first time dealing with death. It sucked, but since then I've been good with coping with loss. I can accept and let go and remember the good times. 6th grade was already dark for me, 7th grade sent me into the repressed state I stayed in for the remainder of high school. I never had a friend group. I had a few friends. Mostly, I had the kids I called my friends in class, but I did not talk in school much. I was too exhausted to do my homework at home usually and would spend my lunch periods and any free time I had in school to cram in homework instead of socializing. I sat with "popular girls" in class and lunch, but I never knew quite where I stood with them, but I guess that's just how teenage girls are. I'll always wonder what it's like to be one of those regular teenage girls, but I'd be dead before I'd let myself become one. I would also sit with "weirdos", I really didn't care, and more importantly just didn't know where I belonged. I still made honor roll every quarter, but I was putting as minimal effort possible into doing so. I was coasting.

I'm happy to say I believe I have done much healing. I do love attending Western, my major, my classes and my professors. I love going to class now. I quit volleyball and haven't had a boyfriend in 2 years and am enjoying doing my own thing and learning more about myself. I have a few close friends and I make new ones everywhere I go now. I got a job bartending down the road from my house. I'm a lot more outgoing and confident, like I used to be when I was younger in elementary school. I travel often and am making Dean's list. I plan to study abroad in France next fall semester. This started a few years ago when I began to try to train myself into thinking positively!

Cierra graduated from Western and is enrolled in the University of Hartford Graduate School majoring in Special Education. Now happily married, she works with young people and serves as a positive, supportive force.

ANNE

I am 16 and "colored" with naturally curly hair.
I reminisce squatting on the floor before school as
mama tried to comb through my kinky hair and I would
always flinch and say, "Don't pull right there!"

Born in the Caribbean Islands, I know my true worth. I am a diamond.
Girls like us are often degraded. With make-up and
fake lashes we often are masqueraded.

"You're pretty for a Black girl," is what I've been told,
but I am plainly confused because all us Black
girls are nothing but beauty and gold.
"Colored girl, what do you feel, see and hear?"
Well, I feel, see, and hear the same things as the white girls,
yet still in the 20th century I don't have the same rights,
I beg to differ and as a Black girl I've put up more of a fight.

Some say ignorance is bliss.
This colored girl is not ignorant, this I can't dismiss.

It's the way I am perceived because their skin is light
And I am a shade closer to that of anthracite.

I like to eat, sleep and shop.
I hear white girls shouting, "Shop till you drop!"
So, what truly makes us different?
It's just society that's ignorant.
Inside I am as Black as the whites
And they are as white as I
To this I do testify.
I witness and just ask why?

About the Author

Born in Brooklyn and raised in Long Island, Andee Nunn received her BA in Speech Education and MS in Secondary Education from Queens College. She completed post-graduate studies in Reading at Western Connecticut State University. In more than 40 years of teaching she reached over 4,000 students juggling positions as a Reading Specialist, English Teacher, and Communication Adjunct Faculty. Nunn's awards include 2008 Danbury Teacher of the Year, 2008 Connecticut State Semi-Finalist Teacher of the Year, and 2018 NAACP Excellence in Teaching. She resides in Danbury, where she raised two daughters, and lives with her husband of 46 years. Her favorite pastime is enjoying visits with her four grandchildren. *Magic in Room 216* is her debut book.